THE REGIONAL GOVERNING OF
METROPOLITAN AMERICA

ESSENTIALS OF PUBLIC POLICY AND ADMINISTRATION SERIES

SERIES EDITOR: Jay Shafritz
University of Pittsburgh

Westview Press proudly announces a new series of textbooks for public policy and administration courses. Written for students at both the advanced undergraduate level and graduate level, these texts follow a standard design and format which allows them to be incorporated easily into multiple courses. Each text covers a core aspect of public policy and administration that is commonly discussed in the classroom. They are written by authorities in their fields, and will serve as both core and supplemental texts.

New titles in the series include:

Managing Diversity in Public Sector Workforces, Norma M. Riccucci
Comparative Public Administration and Policy, Jamil E. Jreisat
The Regional Governing of Metropolitan America, David Y. Miller

THE REGIONAL
GOVERNING OF
METROPOLITAN
AMERICA

David Y. Miller
University of Pittsburgh

Westview
PRESS

A Member of the Perseus Books Group

Copyright © 2002 by Westview Press, A Member of the Perseus Books Group

Westview Press books are available at special discounts for bulk purchases in the United States by corporations, institutions, and other organizations. For more information, please contact the Special Markets Department at The Perseus Books Group, 11 Cambridge Center, Cambridge MA 02142, or call (617) 252-5298.

Published in 2002 in the United States of America by Westview Press, 5500 Central Avenue, Boulder, Colorado 80301–2877, and in the United Kingdom by Westview Press, 12 Hid's Copse Road, Cumnor Hill, Oxford OX2 9JJ

Find us on the World Wide Web at www.westviewpress.com

A Cataloging-in-Publication Data Record is available from the Library of Congress.

ISBN 0-8133-3991-X (hc.)
ISBN 0-8133-9807-X (pbk.)

The paper used in this publication meets the requirements of the American National Standard for Permanence of Paper for Printed Library Materials Z39.48–1984.

10   9   8   7   6   5   4   3   2   1

CONTENTS

v

TABLES AND ILLUSTRATIONS

Charts

ACKNOWLEDGMENTS

Writing the beginning of a book at the end of the process has proved to be a relatively easy task. I say that as I fly over the Atlantic Ocean, returning from a vacation in several European metropolitan regions. The experience has left me with an ever greater sense of the current and emerging importance of metropolitan regions in the United States. It has also left me with a sense of how fundamentally different they are than their European counterparts.

I am indebted to a number of individuals. This book is heavily influenced by systems theory—the notion that processes and components are linked in ways in which the sum of the parts is greater than the whole. A metropolitan region is, indeed, a system that can be conceptualized, studied, and treated as a whole, even though it lacks the political and institutional structure of formal political jurisdictions like nations, states, and cities. For this insight, I am grateful to Alex Weilenmann. I am also even more grateful for his patience in letting me conceptualize systems theory at my own pace, although I now recognize how painfully slow that must have appeared to Alex.

Although I consider myself a social scientist, mathematics has never been one of my stronger subjects. However, in the emerging discipline of the study of metropolitan regions in the United States, I believed we needed a simple and easily understandable way to measure those regions against each other to capture their political structure. It was Bill Matlack who, over coffee, laid out the mathematics of my political theorizing about what I have called the Metropolitan Power Diffusion Index (MPDI).

Breathing life into the MPDI also required someone with the conceptual and technical skills to translate an idea into action. For this role, Chris Briem at the University Center for Social and Urban Research proved invaluable.

Under the adage of failure to see the forest for the trees, I am indebted to Jane Lohman. Her reading of the text and subsequently eliminating many of the idiosyncratic foibles of my writing style has greatly improved the prose. In similar fashion, early versions of the text were helped by my graduate assistant, Amy Camp, and my summer 2001 class on Comparative Regional Governance at the University of Pittsburgh.

Although they all contributed to the final version, the ultimate responsibility for any errors or omissions, factual or conceptual, rests with me.

No work of this magnitude can be accomplished without patience. Lacking that virtue myself, it is to my wife that this responsibility fell. She assumed that role without hesitation as she always has. It is to her that this book is dedicated.

D. Y. M.

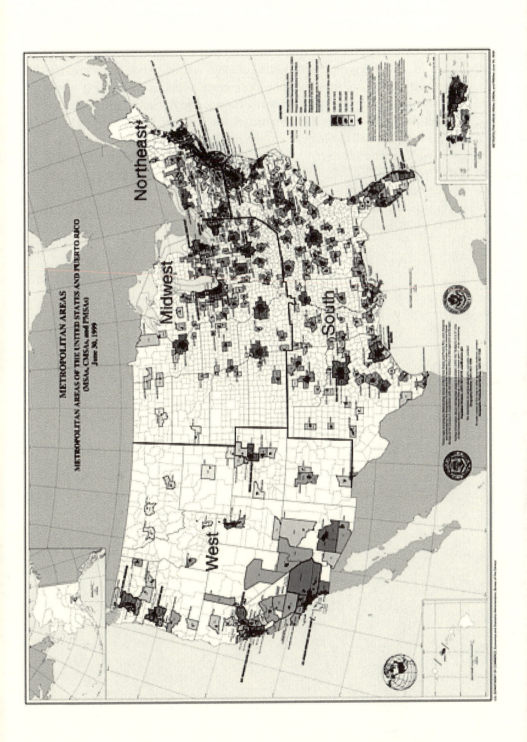

1

Introduction

This book is about the governing of metropolitan regions in the United States. The concept of a metropolitan region is relatively new. Faced with the rapid growth of suburbs, the creation of satellite cities, new modes of transportation, increased mobility of citizens, and easier forms of communication, an academic roundtable on regional planning proposed that a "new political or administrative entity" at the metropolitan level needed to be created that was different from the precinct, ward, municipality, county, or state.[1] The year was 1926. Seventy-one years later, Anthony Downs lamented, "As Congress shifts many federal powers to lower levels of government, it is missing a unique opportunity to resolve a fundamental flaw in America's government structure: the absence of any authority at the metropolitan regional level. Metropolitan regions have become the most important functional units of economic and social life in almost all modern societies" (Downs, 1997).

The road to the metropolitan region takes us through the land of local government. Local governments are the building blocks of the metropolitan regions. The American system of governing and government is best understood as a territorial based distribution of power and responsibility. It is steeped in both law and popular culture. Over 40 years ago, Arthur Maas (1959) defined the structure of local government in the United States as an "areal" division of power wherein the territorial bounded local governments were, by culture and practice, an integral part of a system of organizing that divided power between the federal, state, and local governments. In 1868, Justice Dillon (*City of Clinton v. The Cedar Rapids and Missouri Railroad*) articulated America's legal doctrine on local governments, calling them "mere tenants at will of their respective state legislatures" which could be "eliminated by the legislature with a stroke of the pen." Dillon also articulated America's popular doctrine on local governments by calling such an act (the elimination of a local government) "so great a folly, and so great a wrong." Such is the paradox of local government in United States—so weak, yet so strong.

Thomas Jefferson (quoted in Syed, 1965: 40) called townships "the wisest invention ever devised by the wit of man." Alexis de Tocqueville (1805–1859), a French sociologist reporting back to Europe in 1840 on the new experiment in democracy in America, called the New England towns the real innovation in human organization. He pointed out that the townships "have not been invested with privileges, but they have, on the contrary, forfeited a portion of their independence to the state" (de Tocqueville, 1946: 57). Zuckerman (1970: 46–47) maintains that colonial America used the terms "the people" and "individualism" to mean "the people or individuals aggregated on different principles than those of the centralized state—sovereignty in severalty, the sovereignty of local groups and localities." Wendell Phillips (cited in Hofstadter, 1948: 162), a 19th century American abolitionist and socialist, captured this American vision when he said, "My ideal of a civilization is a very high one; but the approach to it is a New England town of some 2000 inhabitants, with no rich man and no poor man in it, all mingling in the same society, nobody too proud to stand aloof, nobody too humble to be shut out."

This tradition of strong local government is so embedded within the context of the American system that Thomas Reed (1925: 417), when proposing the creation of a new governmental unit he called a metropolitan "region," was quick to point out, "Metropolitan organization . . . must not fly in the face of the traditions and habits of the people, but must leave in existence, to the greatest extent possible, the customary units of local government."

Elazar (1971) suggests that American cultural values create a political system that desires to implement "essentially agrarian ideals in an urban setting." The structuring principle in such an environment is the local community. It leads, according to Elazar, to "the development of a nation of territorially based communities that have the right to maintain and perpetuate legitimate differences, to the extent that their inhabitants so choose, as well as an equal opportunity for access to national resources for their residents." Elsewhere, Elazar (1975: 58) has suggested that the "locus of governmental decision making in the metropolis is independent (local) governments regardless of the dicta of economists or the preaching of reformers."

Compare the above American perspective on territorial based local government systems with commentaries from the British system of governing. Langrod (1953: 29) comments, "The incompatibility of democratic principle with the practice of decentralization is a phenomenon so evident that it may be considered a kind of sociological law." Smith (1985: 4) suggests, "There are differences of opinion as to how necessary local self-government is to the political health of the modern democratic state . . . . territorial interest may be classed among those sectional interests which are seen as incompatible with society's 'general will' represented by the nation's legislature." The conceptual foundation for this more centralized perspective lies with, among others, John Stuart Mill. Adopting the notion of a distinction between power and knowledge, Mill believed that local familiarity with details required that local government be the administrators of local functions, while the general principles of governing ought to be centralized. Mill (1873: 304) stated, "To every branch of local administration which affects the general interest there should be a corresponding central organ." After all, the methods that constitute "good management are the same everywhere; there is no good reason why police, or jails, or the administration of justice should be differently managed in one part of the kingdom and in another part" (Mill, 1873: 300).

America did not adopt the British view of local government and even Britain has debates over such a centralist position. Governance in the metropolitan areas in America is, fundamentally, built around local governments. Although some may argue that presuming the structure of metropolitan areas is built on local government has the effect of limiting the choices of reform, Dillon's words of 150 years ago are as relevant today as ever. Legally and judicially, we could and can do away with local government, but practice and tradition makes that option such a "wrong" and a "folly" that it falls outside the range of reasonable solutions.

In addition to the broad cultural appeal that local government enjoys in the American system, the monopoly position of local governments in two key policy areas makes the assumption a practical reality. The first is local government's exclusive ability to raise public funds through taxation. Although regulated by state governments, this power helps organize how public funds are allocated. The second is local government's exclusive ability to make land use decisions, primarily through the exercise of zoning powers. As with taxation power, this monopoly position is tempered by state regulatory responsibility.

In grounding this book about metropolitan regions on local government, I do not want to convey that I am a "cheerleader" for the existing system of relationships among local governments in metropolitan areas. Indeed, I will demonstrate that those relationships are fundamentally flawed. As such, I suggest that all is not well in America's metropolitan regions. Rather, I want to suggest that there is a movement, albeit painfully slow, toward regional solutions to public problems in those metropolitan areas as homegrown, evolutionary processes. As systems, metropolitan regions are adapting to the changing environment of which they are a part. But that adaptation is occurring paradoxically. At the same time that these systems of local governments are becoming more diffused or decentralized, they are becoming more coordinated. This paradox is possible because most lasting regional approaches emerge as negotiated agreements and understandings between players over time. Externally imposed solutions, although often seen as the visible form of regionalism, seldom work. They are the mere "tip of the iceberg" of activities that could be considered regional.

It is also clear that the need to find new solutions and cooperative relations is often driven by federal and state actions that serve to force the local governments into action. However, those outside influences and the response are interpreted locally.

The emergence of metropolitan governing has occurred within the context of an older system of intergovernmental relations and represents an adaptation of that older system. Our discussion, therefore, starts with that older system of relationships. A model of that traditional system is presented in Figure 1.1. In this simplified presentation, there are four principal actors—the citizen, local governments, state governments, and the federal government. When I use the term "citizen," I mean it in the broadest sense. It is meant to include citizens, local businesses, and other users of services in a metropolitan environment. The term "local governments" is used to broadly define governmental entities such as towns, cities, counties, special districts, and school districts.[2]

Look at Figure 1.1 from the citizen's perspective. "Citizens" receive a bundle of services from their local governments (Y6) and a bundle of services from their state government (Y7). Those services are partially funded by a tax and fee bundle that the citizen pays to their respective state (Y2) and local (Y1) governments. As will be discussed in more detail, the state government also provides significant funding to the local governments (Y3) to undertake a wide variety of activities. The federal government, to the degree that it delivers urban services, provides those services

FIGURE 1.1 The Traditional System of Intergovernmental Relations in Metropolitan Areas

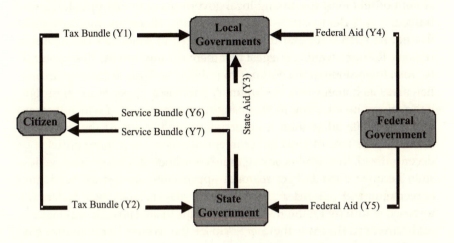

SOURCE: *David Miller*

in the form of financial assistance to state governments (Y5) and to local governments (Y4).

From the local governments' perspective, they receive an allocation of funds from the community (Y1), an allocation of resources from the state (Y3) that may or may not have mandates attached, and an allocation from the federal government (Y4). With those resources, the local governments deliver a bundle of services (Y6) that reflect the interests of their citizens, the state, and the federal government.

From the state's perspective, it receives an allocation of funds from the community (Y2) and a significant allocation of resources from the federal government. With those resources, the state delivers a bundle of services (Y7) directly to the citizens. It also provides an allocation of funds to the local governments in the form of state aid (Y3) to undertake a wide variety of activities. Some of those activities are to administer state programs where the local government is acting as agent for the state. Some of the funding is provided to local governments to undertake locally designed programs.

From the federal perspective, it administers policy through the provision of aid to the state governments (Y5) and to local governments (Y4). I have elected not to draw a line from the citizen to the federal government, although it is obvious that citizens also pay taxes to that government as well. However, for purposes of the metropolitan region, the perceived role of the federal government is limited and somewhat disconnected in the minds of the citizen as it relates to traditional local government services.

Although Figure 1.1 can be universally applied to the United States, we must recognize that there are 50 different and very distinct patterns of relationships—one for each state. Further, it is also important to remember that these state systems have evolved over the last 250 years and, as such, have become so institutionalized and reified that it becomes extremely difficult to make changes and then to perceive those changes as significant.

Also, the system reflects overlapping citizenship. Each citizen is a member of each level of government—local, state, and federal. Each government, in turn, considers, for purposes of its relationship with the citizen, its government to be the primary unit of government.

It is into this rich milieu of relationships that we introduce a new player—the metropolitan region. The concept of metropolitan region is attached onto those existing patterns of relationships, becoming defined by those existing relationships in the process. I have demonstrated this layering of the metropolitan region in Figure 1.2. We understand how the old system works, but we hardly understand the new system at all. I have used the dashed lines and oddly shaped depiction of the metropolitan region to reflect this lack of clarity in our understanding.

For instance, the dashed line from the citizen to the metropolitan region is hardly present, currently, in the system. Few, if any, regions have metropolitan level officials and institutions that are even vaguely known by citizens. The line from state government to the metropolitan region usually goes through institutions of local governments. The line from the federal government to the metropolitan region varies from federal agency to federal agency. One agency of the federal government, the Office of Management and Budget, defines metropolitan regions, but then warns against using those definitions for any application but statistical applications. Conversely, the Department of Transportation has forced the flow of federal highway dollars through a metropolitan regional organization, generally utilizing the definitions supplied by the Office of Management and Budget.

Understanding how the innovation (metropolitan region) affects the existing perspective of the state, or the feds, or the citizen, or the local governments is the objective of this book.

FIGURE 1.2   The Emerging System of Intergovernmental Relations in Metropolitan Areas

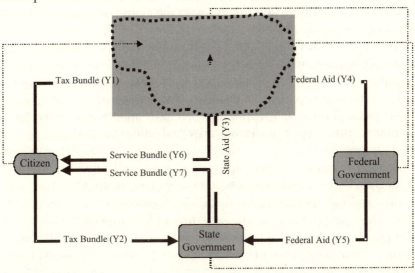

SOURCE: *David Miller*

The organization of this book is designed to explore the regional governing of metropolitan America in a systematic fashion. In Chapter 2, we will review the financial system of state and local government at the broadest possible level—the national level. We will see the fundamental relationships between the federal government, the 50 state governments, and the 86,000 local governments that constitute the United States system. In Chapter 3, we will focus on defining local government. There are several types of local government that have fundamentally different purposes, organizational designs, and powers. Local government includes counties, municipalities (both cities and towns), and special districts.

Chapter 4 will focus on what limited knowledge we have about metropolitan regions. Although defined for statistical purposes by the federal government, metropolitan areas have emerged as a tool that can be used to begin to understand how metropolitan regions throughout the United States are responding to the governance needs of their areas. In Chapter 5, we will compare and contrast variations in the design of metropolitan systems throughout the United States. I will introduce the Metropolitan Power Diffusion Index (MPDI), a scale that assesses the distribution of local government power at the metropolitan level.

In Chapter 6, we will overview the classic debate over how metropolitan areas in the United States ought to be organized. One view, which I called the "region as organic whole," sees the metropolitan region as formally organized to explicitly serve the purposes of the region as it competes with other metropolitan regions throughout the world in pursuit of economic development. The second view, which I called the "polycentric region," views the metropolitan region as a diverse set of personal choices in which citizens choose to reside in places that match their personal preferences. Global competitiveness results from creating an environment that encourages private enterprise and entrepreneurship.

In Chapter 7, we will look in detail at regional strategies that have been developed to govern the metropolitan areas of the United States. These strategies can be loosely bundled into what has commonly come to be known as "metropolitan regionalism." Regionalism occurs when two or more local governments or communities within a metropolitan region work in some coordinated fashion on one or more issues of public policy. I will present four types of metropolitan regionalism. Those types are coordinating, administrative, fiscal, and structural. Each of these strategies can be found to one degree or another in each of the metropolitan regions in the United States.

In Chapter 8, we will explore problems or issues that arise as a result of the structuring of government systems in metropolitan areas. We will pay particular attention to the issues of racial segregation and fiscal equity between jurisdictions.

I admit to having a strong historical bias in the presentation of this material. The American local government system has evolved through the act of the doing of community life over the last three hundred or so years. I have gone down some of those pathways of history throughout the book. It is that history that drove us, rightly or wrongly, to where we are today. In a like fashion, that historical context frames and structures where we are headed. The old adage fits, "We cannot know where we are headed unless we know where we have been."

Notes

1. Roundtable on Regional Planning. (1926). *American Political Science Review.* Volume XX, 156–163

2. Garn and Springer (1975) introduce the notion of economic clubs that are formed for either the purpose of production and/or consumption of goods and services. Whether in the private or public sector, the purpose for clubs formation is the same: benefit maximization, cost minimization, and association. Political

units can be seen as clubs of clubs. Conceptualizing metropolitan areas and local governments within those areas as clubs for clubs of clubs acknowledges that actions taken by particular clubs will affect other clubs in such a way as to change the benefit-costs-association for those clubs. This notion has led to conceptualizing local governments as growth machines, fiercely competing with each other based on the interest of the "clubs" to constitute each of those governments (Orum, 1991; Peterson, 1979, 1981).

2

Financial Overview of the State and Local Governments System

State and local government in America is big business. In 1996, state and local governments received and spent $1.551 trillion and employed close to 15,000,000 individuals. On the revenue side, state governments raised or charged $553 billion and received $221 billion in intergovernmental transfers—$208 billion in the form of federal aid. Local governments raised or charged $508 billion and received $271 billion in intergovernmental transfers—$27 billion in the form of federal aid and $244 in the form of state aid (see Figure 2.1).

The dynamic interrelationship between states and local governments is highlighted when expenditure data is reviewed. Whereas, in 1996, state governments spent on operations $511 billion, local governments spent nearly 60 percent more—$778 billion. The difference is primarily a function of state aid, reflecting the dual nature of local governments: that of administrator of state programs and that of provider of locally originated and financed programming. Another way to conceptualize the system is to view the major role of the state as that of revenue generator, while the major role of local government can best be typified as service provider.

Because revenues and expenditures paint different but interrelated pictures of the state and local government system, I will treat each separately.

State and Local Revenues

In 1996, over 88 percent of state tax revenues ($369 billion) were collected through sales and income taxes. Conversely, 74 percent of local tax

FIGURE 2.1   The 1996 State and Local Government System

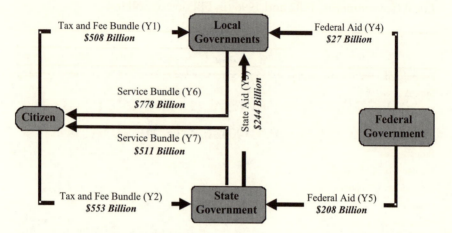

SOURCE: *U.S. Department of Commerce, Bureau of Census:*
http://ww.census.gov/govs/estimate/96s+lus.txt

revenues ($199 billion) were from the property tax. The dedication of particular types of revenues to particular levels of government has historical roots. When new communities were developing in the 18th century, those communities had need for a set of public services generally related to property—roads needed to be built to the new settlements, property needed to be protected through police and fire services, a system was needed to define where one's property ended and the neighbor's property began. The amount of land one owned was a fairly reliable measure of one's wealth, such that a tax on the value of property served the purpose of raising public dollars fairly and equitably while being used for property related services. As a result, property taxes became the domain of local governments. State governments, primarily delivering non-property related services, developed a tax base not connected to property.

Comparing and contrasting sources of local government revenues between 1982 and 1996 reveals a fairly stable picture. In 1982, property taxes constituted 76 percent of local government tax revenues. In 1996, property taxes made up 74 percent of local government tax revenues. Although often maligned as an unfair and difficult tax to administer, the property tax continues to dominate as the primary source of revenue for local governments. To the degree that local governments have looked to other tax revenue sources, the sales tax is the tax of choice. Whereas sales taxes constituted 14 percent of 1982 local government tax revenues, they

TABLE 2.1   Comparison of Principal Revenue Sources for State and Local Governments, 1982 and 1996 (in billions of dollars)

	FY 1996			FY 1982		
	Total	*State*	*Local*	*Total*	*State*	*Local*
Federal Aid	235	208	27	87	66	21
State Aid	244	0	244	92	0	92
Local Government Aid	13	13	0	-	-	-
Sales Tax	249	206	43	94	79	15
Property Tax	209	10	199	82	3	79
Income Tax - Individuals[a]	147	134	13	51	46	5
Income Tax - Corporate	32	29	3			
Other Taxes	38	27	11	34	29	5
Motor Vehicle Licenses	14	13	1	6	6	0
Total Tax Collections	689	418	271	266	163	104
Hospitals	51	16	35			
Education	50	38	12			
Sewerage	21	0	21			
Solid Waste	9	0	9			
All Other Current Charges	52	14	38			
Total Current Charges	182	67	115	-	-	-
Utility Revenues	72	4	68	-	-	-
Interest Earnings	58	29	29	6	3	3
Misc Revenues	59	35	24	30	12	18
General Operating Revenues	1,551	774	777	482	243	238

[a] 1982 data includes individual and corporate tax revenue

SOURCE: *U.S. Department of Commerce, Bureau of Census: Census of Governments: Finance Summary Statistics: http://ww.census.gov/govs/estimate/96s+lus.txt*

were 16 percent of 1996 total tax revenues. Rather than relying on shifting tax revenue sources, local governments have been more likely to look to user fees for additional revenues, a topic that will be discussed later.

State governments were more apt to concentrate their tax revenues in sales and income taxes in 1996 than they were in 1982. Whereas those sources constituted 88 percent of 1996 collections, they were only 77 percent of 1982 collections.

One of the more interesting revenue trends is the rate of overall tax growth when comparing state and local revenues. State governments, relying on progressive taxes (sales and income) which are elastic and, therefore, more likely to expand as the economy expands, grew 157 percent (from $163 billion to $418 billion) over the period 1982 to 1996. Meanwhile, local governments, relying on the more inelastic property tax, saw those property taxes grow by 161 percent (from $104 billion to $271 billion) during the same period. Although beleaguered and condemned, the property tax continues to dominate the local government revenue picture and demonstrates remarkable capacity to grow and expand.

User fees or charges for current services are primarily the domain of local governments. In 1996, local governments collected 63 percent of all current charges and 95 percent of all utility revenues. State government charges are primarily in the area of higher education—56 percent of state current charges are related to that area. In the areas of hospitals, sewerage, solid waste, and other activities, local governments are the dominant revenue collectors.

The revenue area that has experienced the most significant change over the last several years is intergovernmental transfers. The 1960s and 1970s were highlighted by an increasing involvement of the federal government in the direct financing of local government. In 1982, 24 percent ($21 billion of $87 billion) of federal aid to state and local governments went to local governments. The mid 1980s saw retrenchment on the part of the federal government in the financing of local governments. By 1996, local governments received 11 percent ($27 billion of $235 billion) of total federal distribution to state and local governments.

The withdrawal of the federal government from direct support of local governments is sharply contrasted with a significant expansion of its support of state governments. Whereas federal aid to local governments grew by only 27 percent, federal aid to state governments grew by 215 percent. Although an internal shift of federal aid occurred, federal aid as a percent of total state and local tax revenues has remained relatively constant—33 percent in 1982 and 34 percent in 1996.

The relationship between the federal government, the state governments and local governments needs some historical context. The federal system in the United States, as embodied in the Constitution, is an agreement in the form of a contract between the federal government and the states. The word "federal" is derived from the Latin, *foedus*, which means contract. As part of that contract, the internal affairs of the constituent states are reserved for the states to decide. Local governments fall within the purview of the states. Hence, the federal government's link to local governments has always been a tenuous one that is, at best, indirect. The perceived urban crisis of the 1960s and 1970s helped to change temporarily that historical relationship and led to a brief period where the federal government took a much greater direct financial role in local government. This new engagement of the federal government in local affairs was highlighted by a program that operated during the 1970s and early 1980s called "General or Federal Revenue Sharing," wherein literally every general purpose local government in America received an annual formula-driven allocation from the federal government. The experiment of federal involvement in local government, including Federal Revenue Sharing, ended in the mid 1980s.

Over sixty-five percent of local government revenues are collected through local governments assessing a tax, charging a fee, or otherwise relying on raising the money themselves. I refer to these revenues as "own-source" revenues. Although a two-edged sword, this reliance on own-source revenues is a significant and defining feature of the American system in contrast to most other systems of local government in the world. On one hand, it is one of the most significant empowering features of the system. It allows communities to decide, locally, which issues are important enough to allocate resources. It creates ownership in the process of governing in that no higher level of government is telling communities what to do or is providing resources so that needs are met through "someone else's money." On the other hand, it sets in motion a potentially dangerous and fiercely competitive battle between governments. If the local decisions to raise own-source revenues create a tax and fee package that is not competitive with other communities' tax and fee packages, disinvestments and flight from the non-competitive community set in motion a downward economic spiral for that community.

State and Local Expenditures

Turning to the other side of the financial ledger, a review of expenditures reveals distinct differences in the functions performed by state and local governments (see Table 2.2). A point worth repeating is that local government is the primary service deliverer. In 1996, for every dollar spent by state governments in service delivery, local governments spent $1.52.

State governments concentrated 63.1 percent of their 1996 spending in two program areas—social services and education. The former, social ser-

TABLE 2.2   Comparison of Principal Expenditures for State and Local Governments, 1982 and 1996 (in billions of dollars)

	FY 1996			FY 1982		
	Total	State	Local	Total	State	Local
Education	399	107	292	143	31	112
Social Services	308	216	92	82	59	23
Public Safety	115	37	78	35	10	25
Transportation	92	49	42	34	19	15
Environment/Community	103	21	82	27	6	21
Other	118	49	70	25	9	16
Administration	62	25	37	22	8	14
Utilities	93	8	84	15	2	13
General Operating Expenditures	1289	511	778	383	144	239

SOURCE: *U.S. Department of Commerce, Bureau of Census. Census of Governments: Finance Summary Statistics. 1982 and 1996*

vices, accounted for 42.2 percent ($216 billion) of total state spending. Although state governments spent only 39.7 percent of combined state and local expenditures, state governments spent 70 percent of total state and local government social services expenditures ($308 billion). The latter program area, education (primarily post-high-school higher education), accounted for 20.9 percent ($107 billion) of total state spending.

Local government spending is more diverse. Topping the list of local services is education. Education expenditures in 1996 constituted 37.6 percent of local government expenditures and are concentrated primarily at the elementary and secondary levels. Expenditures by local governments in education represent 73.3 percent of combined state and local expenditures.

Social services constitute the next highest category of local government expenditures. In 1992, they made up $92 billion (12 percent) of all local government expenditures. When education expenditures are combined with social services expenditures, they account for 49 percent of total local government expenditures.

Another 31.4 percent of local government expenditures are made in more traditional property related services. The list includes: utilities (sewer, water, energy), accounting for 10.9 percent ($84 billion); environmental and community expenditures, accounting for 10.5 percent ($82 billion); public safety expenditures, accounting for 10.0 percent ($78 billion) and transportation, accounting for 5 percent ($42 billion). In these

TABLE 2.3 Distribution of Principal Expenditures by Level of Government, 1982 and 1996

	State and Local		State		Local	
	1996	1982	1996	1982	1996	1982
Education	30.9	37.3	20.9	21.3	37.6	46.9
Social Services	23.9	21.4	42.2	40.7	11.9	9.8
Public Safety	8.9	9.1	7.1	6.8	10.0	10.4
Transportation	7.1	8.8	9.6	13.4	5.5	6.1
Environment/Community	8.0	7.1	4.1	4.4	10.5	8.8
Other	9.2	6.6	9.5	6.5	9.0	6.6
Administration	4.8	5.8	4.9	5.8	4.8	5.8
Utilities	7.2	3.9	1.6	1.1	10.9	5.5
General Expenses	100.0	100.0	100.0	100.0	100.0	100.0

SOURCE: *U.S. Department of Commerce, Bureau of Census. Census of Governments: Finance Summary Statistics. 1982 and 1996*

four areas, local governments make 71 percent of total state and local government expenditures.

The administration category loosely covers the cost of administration or overhead of the system. Its sub-categories include: "financial administration," "judicial administration," "general public buildings," and "other government administration." It represents 4.8 percent of total state expenditures and 4.9 percent of total local government expenditures.

State expenditures grew more rapidly than local government expenditures between 1982 and 1996. Overall, state expenditures grew by 255 percent while local government expenditures increased by 225 percent. This increase in state spending was primarily a function of social service expenditures. State governments increased expenditures in social services by 269 percent during that period.

The expenditure data is summarized in Table 2.3. This table demonstrates the shifts in expenditure priorities that occurred over the latter part of the 20th century. In 1982, 37.3 percent of state and local government expenditures were for education. By 1996, that percentage had decreased to 30.9 percent. Areas of spending that had experienced increased priority included utilities (from 3.9 percent to 7.2 percent), social services (from 21.4 percent to 23.9 percent), environment and community services (from 7.1 percent to 8.0 percent) and other expenditures (from 6.6 percent to 9.1 percent).

Summary

Revenues and expenditures paint an important but partial picture of the governance system in the United States. The distribution of personnel also reflects the local nature of the delivery system. In 1995, there were 1,790,000 full-time-equivalent employees (FTE) in federal non-defense agencies. State governments employed 3,951,000. Those numbers pale in comparison to the 10,016,000 employed at the local government level (Stephens and Wikstrom, 1999: 23). Even when defense employees are added to the federal government numbers, local government employment is still twice that of the federal government.

The employment trend suggests that dependency on local government delivery of domestic services will continue. Between 1952 and 1995, federal government non-defense employment rose by 47.2 percent while local government employment rose by 189.4 percent.

In summary, the state and local government system in the United States has evolved specialized roles for states and their constituent local governments. State governments are the primary revenue generator for the system and they rely heavily on sales and income taxes. States deliver services, primarily in the areas of social services and higher education. States are the primary recipient of federal aid. States also provide significant funding in the form of aid to local governments. As such, states use local governments as administrators of some of their programs.

Local governments are the primary service providers and they rely heavily on their own source revenues, primarily in the form of property taxes and user fees. Not only do local governments directly deliver more programs than states, those programs tend to be more diverse with a focus on education and property related services. Local governments no longer receive substantial direct support of the federal government. They do receive significant contributions from state governments to support operations. This state aid serves two purposes. It can be used to administer state programs or as funds that are general purpose in nature to help local governments administer locally defined programs.

3

Defining Types of Local Government

Not all local governments are alike. There are three primary forms of local government.[1] The first is the county. The second is the municipality, although there is a certain liberty I am taking given the different forms that are found in the American states. There are two primary types of municipality—the township and the city. The third form of local government is the special district. A particular variant of a special district, the school district, sometimes looks more like a municipality than a special district, and therefore will be treated separately.

The American system of local government features many governments. In 1997, as demonstrated in Table 3.1, there were 87, 453 local governments in the United States. Between 1952 and 1997, the overall number of local governments declined. That decline is misleading inasmuch as consolidation and closing of "one-room" schools occurred, particularly in the 50s and 60s. At the same time small schools were closing or consolidating, the growth of special districts accelerated, representing one of the most significant trends in local government administration in the United States. Since 1952, over 22,000 new special districts have been created. In addition, over 2,000 new municipal governments have been created during the same period. To put those numbers in perspective, there have been approximately 500 new local governments created in America each year for the last 45 years.

Through most of the 20th century, the number of county governments has remained virtually unchanged. Historically, state governments created county governments as a means by which the state administered its functions, primarily judicial. As a result, county governments were laid out at roughly the same time a state was formed. There were 3,062 county

TABLE 3.1   Number of Governments by Type, 1997

	1952	1967	1987	1997	Change 1952 to 1997	
					Number	Percent
Counties	3,049	3,049	3,042	3,043	(6)	−0.2
Municipal – City	16,778	18,048	19,200	19,372	2,594	15.5
Municipal – Town	17,202	17,105	16,691	16,629	(573)	−3.3
District – School	56,346	21,742	14,721	13,726	(42,620)	−75.6
District – Special	12,319	21,264	29,532	34,683	22,364	181.5
All Governments	105,694	81,208	83,186	87,453	(18,241)	−17.3

SOURCE: *U.S. Departmnt of Commerce, Bureau of Census. Volume 1: Governmental Organization*

governments in 1932 and 3,043 in 1997. It is unlikely that change in the number of county governments will occur in the future.

Primarily for international readers, I need to clarify the relationship between the various types of local governments. In most states with counties, all other forms of local government usually are nested geographically within the boundaries of a county. It is easy to interpret that structure to presume that states are made up of counties that, in turn, are made up of municipalities. In such an arrangement, municipalities are presumed to report to counties that report to states. Even though local governments are located within a county, there is no hierarchical relationship between county government and local governments. The structural organization of local governments is portrayed in Figure 3.1. Under existing law, all counties, all municipalities and independent school districts are creatures of their respective state. Some special districts and dependent school districts are creatures of their respective county or municipal government. In law, these districts are, literally, "wholly-owned subsidiaries" of those governments. Some dependent school districts are not even a subsidiary but a department within the municipal or county government. Other special districts are separate and distinct from municipal or county governments and are truly independent governments.

As is the case with most pronouncements on the governance structure of America, there are exceptions. Such is the case with special districts. Because state legislatures can create and abolish units of local government, they can also create special districts. As a result, some special dis-

FIGURE 3.1 The Organizational Structure of Local Government in America

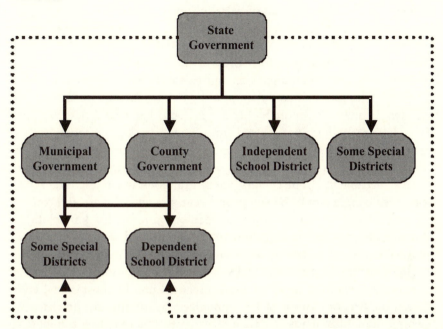

SOURCE: *David Miller*

tricts report directly to the state, circumventing local control. For instance, in Allegheny County, Pennsylvania, the state legislature created a special taxing body in 1995 called the Regional Asset District. It legislatively mandated the nature and structure of this organization.

In this chapter we will look at each type of local government in more detail. After that review, we will assess the distribution of functions across those governments. Let us start with the county.

County Government

Geographically, the largest units of local government are counties. County governments exist in all states but Connecticut and Rhode Island. The term "county" includes those entities called "boroughs" in Alaska and "parishes" in Louisiana.

Two distinct images of counties have emerged as part of the American political system. Generally, in New England and, to a lesser degree, the middle-Atlantic states, where towns and villages, even in rural settings, were the primary organizing unit, county government was seen as a sub-division of the state or colony. Shortly after Independence, the newly formed states divided into administrative units (counties) for purposes of delivering state-level services. As a result, counties were not self-consti-tuted governments and became, in the minds of local inhabitants, a more remote and less interesting form of local government.

In the South, where larger scale agricultural development was more prevalent, the county was more apt to be the primary unit of local gov-ernment in all but the more highly developed urban centers (Adrian and Fine, 1991). Although not formed from the bottom up, designation as a county seat represented a significant economic opportunity for a number of communities. Communities lucky enough to be designated the "coun-ty seat" became the trade centers, the central point where the local polit-ical elites congregated, the site of the year's biggest event—the county fair, and the place of institutional memory for the local inhabitants through its record-keeping function (Adrian and Fine, 1991: 180). Particularly in rural areas, county government served as the access point for most citizens to governmental services and opportunities.

This stark contrast in the fundamental building blocks of local civil society in America can best be dramatized by comparing practices in Georgia and Massachusetts. Georgia is representative of a number of southern states that employed the "county unit system" (Marando and Thomas, 1977). In this system, each county was entitled to at least one representative in the state legislature. This organizing principle elevated the importance of county government in the state political process and afforded rural constituencies a far greater role in state policy than they would have had otherwise. In Massachusetts, towns constituted the Colonial Congress. Zuckerman (1970: 20) asserts that such a constitution had the effect of reducing the [State] House of Representatives to a virtu-al congress of communities and establishing a town's "inalienable right to representation." Such a relationship in Massachusetts led Tocqueville (1953: 57) to comment, "It is important to remember that they [the town-ships of New England] have not been vested with privileges, but that they have, on the contrary, forfeited a portion of their independence to the state." Indeed, early deputies to the state legislature were actually town employees and paid by those towns (Zuckerman, 1970).

County governments have a checkered past. They have been referred to as the "dark continent of American politics" (Gilbertson, 1917) and the "forgotten government" (Marando and Thomas, 1977). James Bryce (1922: 605) captured the predominant academic notion of the role of county government when he said, "the system which prevails in the Southern States need not long detain us, for it is less instructive and has proved less successful. Here the unit is the county." Thomas and Marando (1977) note that power concentration in the North is usually referred to as a more value-neutral "city hall" while similar concentration of power in the South is referred to as a heavily value-laden "courthouse gang."

Bryce's impact, among others, has led to an academic lack of respect for county government as a fundamental institution within the American governmental system. There are three reasons for this image. Initially, this relegation to footnote status may have more to do with the way in which county governments are managed and the functions they undertake as opposed to their relevance as units of local governments. When urban problems attract the attention of the nation, it is city government and city mayors that are called upon to address those issues. While city governments are dealing with important problems like terrorism and poverty, county governments have been left to address other less interesting and less important issues like the tarring of county roads. Further, county governments often reflect the rural/suburban constituency of a territory and stand in contrast to the willingness of the city governments to deal with those urban problems. As a result, the image of county government as a sleepy, patronage-riddled organization resistant to change is frequently reinforced in the eyes of the public.

Second, one of the theoretical bases for the organizing of metropolitan areas focuses on drawing boundaries around the smallest relevant service area for the delivery of a particular public good. This theory, sometimes referred to as public choice, relegates county governments to "not critical" status in the governance of metropolitan America. Indeed, they are merely "another potential supplier of urban services, along with special districts, municipalities, and private firms" (Schneider and Park, 1989: 345). Although Schneider and Park go on to demonstrate that urban counties are playing an increasingly important role in the delivery of public goods in urban areas, the image within the theoretical framework of public choice serves to minimize the significance of that role.

Third, and perhaps the most significant reason for the lack of positive image of county government rests in its existing structure and its general unwillingness to change that structure. The primary structure of county government is the commission. Tracing its origins to Pennsylvania in the early 1700s, this structure is little changed and still the predominant form for over 2,500 of the nation's 3,000 counties (Blair, 1986: 105). Under

the commission form of government, the legislative and executive functions are concentrated in a small, elected board, usually referred to as the
Board of County Commissioners. In some states, this board even has
some judicial powers.

In addition to the Board, many of the administrative functions of the
county are handled through a separate set of elected officials, commonly
referred as row officers. For instance, in Pennsylvania, most counties elect
most or all of the following: a district attorney, who serves as the chief
criminal prosecutor; a clerk of courts, who serves as the chief record-
keeper of the criminal courts; a controller, who serves as the financial
watch-dog of the county finances; a coroner, who serves as the chief medical examiner in determining causes of death in suspected criminal cases;
several jury commissioners, who serve as coordinators of lists of citizens
for jury selection; a prothonotary, who serves as the chief record-keeper
of the civil courts; a recorder of deeds, who serves as the administrator of
the deeds records system; a clerk of orphan court, who serves as the chief
record-keeper of the orphan courts; a register of wills, who maintains
jurisdiction over the probating of wills; a sheriff,[2] who serves as the officer of the court; and a treasurer, who collects the revenues (primarily
taxes) for the county.

The term "row office" originates from the physical structure of most
courthouses. Upon walking into a courthouse, lined neatly in a row
with a sign appropriately above the door would be each of the offices.
Legend has it that President Harry Truman, upon entering the courthouse in either Allegheny or Fayette County, Pennsylvania, looked up
at the signs and said what everyone else was thinking, "What the hell is
a prothonotary?" Indeed, Truman's frustration captures the public's
general confusion over county government. Not only is a prothonotary
an obscure administrative position, the public is asked to choose
between two candidates for a position they can hardly understand or
even pronounce. Yet row officers, in most states, are elected officials
with considerable patronage power as well as an ability to thwart the
interest of the commissioners who are more broadly elected to represent
the interests of the public.

In theory, the structure of most county governments reflects an idealized notion of citizen government. The commissioners serve as both
legislators and administrators, making sure the interest of the citizens are
protected, while the election of the row officers guarantees closeness of
the administration to the public. In practice, particularly in more urbanized areas, this structure has led to the image of inaction, patronage, and
irrelevant elected offices.

The primary direction of reform of county government's structure has been to move toward creating a single executive officer, either elected or appointed (Blair, 1986: 107). The elected executive plan was first adopted in 1893 in Cook County, Illinois and now covers more than 60 of the larger county governments. Overall, it is estimated that 480 county governments are organized in this manner (Hansell, 2000: 18). It is most prevalent in New York (where it is referred to as the Supervisor form), in Maryland, and in Wisconsin. Blair (1986: 109) suggests the advantages of the elected executive include a more visible policymaking process for voters to see, the potential for strong political leadership to unite diverse segments of the county, an ability to focus responsibility and accountability for the voters, the potential for increased prestige within the intergovernmental hierarchy, and a more understandable system of checks and balances between the executive and the legislature. Its critics, particularly in light of an historical culture of patronage in many counties, see the concentration of power in the executive as too great an opportunity for bossism.

The appointed executive plan was first introduced in Iredell County, North Carolina in 1927. In this form of government, either the Board of Commissioners or a County Council holds the legislative powers, while the executive authority is vested in a single individual appointed by the legislative body. Currently, over 300 counties have positions that are recognized by the International City and County Management Association (ICMA) as generally meeting the requirements[3] of the single executive. Over 60 percent of those recognized counties are located in the South.

In addition, there are a number of counties that have chief administrative officers who probably meet some parts of the definitional requirements for single executive structure. Blair (1986, 107) estimates the total number of county governments with this form of county government at about 500. A more current estimate is 1,151 (Hansell, 2000: 18).

Nonetheless, approximately 2200 county governments, or 72 percent, retain the traditional structure of county government, the commission, as their organizational design (Hansell, 2000: 18).

Municipal Governments

Municipal governments include townships and cities in most states. Pennsylvania, in addition to towns and cities, also has municipalities called "boroughs." We will explore each of these forms of local government in some detail. Following that discussion, we will review the principal organizational structures for municipal governments.

Generally, there are two images of municipal governments. The first is positive and views local governments as civic communities empowering their citizens to engage in the making of important decisions about the social world in which they live (Elazar, 1966; 1971). The second is a more critical view. Burns (1994) argues that the formation of municipalities is an expensive process, time-consuming, and not always successful. Given these constraints, it takes a combination of citizen interest and business interests to mobilize the resources necessary to be successful. Consequently, business interests, particularly developers and manufacturers, have been more often the drivers of the process. These business interests are searching for favorable regulatory and tax climates and mechanisms that increase land value with minimal risk to developers. When business interests team up with middle and upper middle-class citizens whose interests, in addition to low taxes, are the acquisition of services without having to address the poor and the ability to practice racial exclusion, a coalition is formed that has the staying power and interests to see that the new government is formed.

Township Government

As defined by the Bureau of Census, township government includes towns in the six New England states, Minnesota, New York and Wisconsin, and townships in eleven other states. However, this definition lacks practical meaning as township government defies easy categorization. On one hand, as is the case with the New England towns, they are the foundation from which many local governments in the United States sprang. On the other hand, as is the case in many midwestern states, they are mere shells of institutions, barely worth more than a footnote.

Even though they are seen as important institutions, traditional textbooks follow the Census Bureau and consider the New England towns as different than cities with substantially less power (Zimmerman, 1970; Adrian and Fine, 1991; Halloway, 1951). For purposes of statistical presentation, I retain that distinction. However, New England towns often exercise more discretionary authority then most cities (Zimmerman, 1983). I started my career as a town manager in a small community in Maine called Dover-Foxcroft. Upon entering the town, one is greeted with the sign that says "Incorporated, 1769." This town of 4,500 people owns and operates its own hospital, airport, and several industrial parks. Such a community embodies the notion of local government, whether its title is "city" or "town."

A better way to distinguish between types of municipalities is to consider whether the community was created as an act by the local inhabitants to be a duly constituted civil society or whether the territory was created as a means of subdividing the state or colony. Such self-constituted communities can be officially cities, New England towns, or boroughs, as they are referred to in Pennsylvania.

Outside New England, townships generally fall into two groups (Blair, 1985). Both groups share in common their origins as "congressional townships" that were laid out, starting in 1787, as square six-by-six mile subdivisions by congressional order (Adrian and Fine, 1991). In eight states, the governments of the township are based on the principle of the New England town meeting in which the legislative body of the town is any qualified voter who attends the duly called town meetings of the community. However, this structure is mandated by the legislature and the townships have far fewer powers than those of the New England towns on which they are based.

The townships in seven other states are more like miniature county governments (Blair, 1985). The governing body, usually a board of supervisors or township commissioners, serves as legislature, executive, and often as employees of the town, operating the snowplows in the winter and the tar truck in the summer.

City Government

The second type of municipality is the city. City government includes cities, boroughs (except in Alaska), villages, and towns (except in the six New England states, Minnesota, New York and Wisconsin). Composite city-county governments are also treated as a city government.

Generally, city governments are considered corporate entities. The act of incorporation implies that some part of the local community desired to empower itself to exercise local self-government. This local desire to take on local government responsibility is unlike county governments and the previously mentioned townships. These governments were created by the state to undertake state functions and derive their powers as a subdivision and, as such, are top-down institutions. City governments derive their power from an act of incorporation and, as such, are bottom-up institutions.

Treating city governments in the United States as corporations is based on English tradition. How municipalities became corporations and not associations is a fascinating story (Frug, 1999: 36–38). As Europe emerged from the dark ages, the nation-state, as an organizational innovation, began replacing a society of loosely organized walled cities and rural fiefdoms. The growth of the centralized nation-state in the face of pre-existing decentralized institutions like cities created a tension that had to be resolved. An arrangement, wherein the supremacy of the nation-state was established while retaining an important role for the city, was necessary. As Frug (1999) suggests, political thinkers of the Renaissance conceptualized the existence of real elements of society as the individual and the sovereign (state). Society was formed through a contract between individuals and ruled by a sovereign. By definition, all other elements of society were not real. They were artificial and mere conveniences created for purposes of furthering the objectives of the real elements of society—the individual or the sovereign. As artifacts, these institutions had to be either an extension of individuals or an extension of the sovereign (state). In medieval times, institutions such as the church, the guilds, and the cities were perceived as important intermediary bodies standing between the individual and the state.

An important question, in the development of political theory, was whether cities were extensions of the sovereign or the individual. To have cities as extensions of the individual would have the effect of insulating those cities from the power of the state and minimizing the ability of the nation-state to centralize power. Consider such a relationship to be one of association. Generally, in law, we consider our right to associate or to create an association as a fundamental right of the individual. Indeed, the dictionary definition of an association is an "organization of people with a common purpose." The separation of church and state is an example of the right of the individual to associate freely and without state interference. Churches are extensions of the individual and, as such, are self-regulated through processes determined virtually exclusively by the members of the association.

Conversely, a corporation has a slightly different relationship with the state. Although, as I will discuss later, corporations can and are often as insulated from the state as associations, they, nonetheless, have the distinction of official sanction or creation by the state. Indeed, the dictionary definition of a corporation is "an association of individuals *created by law* and existing as an entity with powers and liabilities independent of those of its members" (italics added). The operative element of the definition is that it is brought into existence by the state.

Initially, the solution, for early nation-building purposes, was to charter or incorporate cities by the nation-state. For instance, the Magna Charta, adopted in 1215, is a grant of power from the sovereign in the form of a license. Although those powers granted in the early city charters were irrevocable and afforded significant municipal autonomy, the city allowed itself to be perceived as something created by the nation-state. With the continued consolidation of power by the nation-state, the state was able to define and manage that which it had created. Particularly in the European context, the corporate status of cities became translated into a hierarchical relationship between the nation-state and the city.

The American context for the development of local government was very different than the European experience. Even though life on the frontier was probably as threatening and dangerous as Europe in the late dark ages, individuals seeking self-constituted religious and mercantile associations primarily undertook European expansion into North America. Indeed, colonization occurred with little sense of central authority and a much stronger sense of the associational relationship formed by compacts between individuals. For instance, the Massachusetts Bay Colony was governed by the rules between the inhabitants laid out in the Mayflower Compact. However, given the knowledge of European tradition held by the colonists, the associational relationship that existed in practice was to be translated into law as incorporation. American towns and cities became corporations even though those corporations were understood to be associations. Zuckerman (1971: 46–47) captures this relationship when he suggests, "After the Revolution, Americans would grope for terms in which to describe this new fact of the dispersal of authority. They [Colonial Americans] would speak of the people and individualism when they meant merely the people or individuals aggregated on different principles than those of the centralized state, when what they really meant was sovereignty of local groups and localities."

Political ideology at the time of the American Revolution was hardly concerned with the distinction between local government as a corporation or an association. Indeed, all corporations were seen as the same. Whether the corporation was a municipality or a business enterprise was immaterial. Municipalities often owned the local taverns, built railroads, and engaged in activities that they defined as appropriate.

The early 19th century saw a growing concern with the notion of a unitary definition of corporation. There emerged a sense that there were different forms of corporations. As Frug (1999) suggests, American political theorists broadly adopted the notion that society was a contract between individuals and governed by a sovereign (the legislature). American political theory was also heavily influenced by the writings of John Locke. Locke postulated that society is formed by individuals who come together and concede only enough of their individual sovereignty as is necessary to preserve and enhance their property. Frug's insightful analysis suggests that this American concern for property served as the basis for classifying corporations. When corporations act to enhance the individual's property, they are acting as an extension of the individual and are private. As private corporations, they are free to advance the interests of the individual with minimal involvement from the state. Indeed, the role of the state is to create the proper environment for the private corporation to pursue its associational interests. Conversely, when corporations act as threats to property, such as taxing property or using eminent domain, they act as extensions of the state and are public. This public domain, in European tradition, was reserved for the sovereign.

American local government in the early 19th century was viewed as either type of corporation. When it acted with property it owned, it was acting as a private corporation, entitled to all of the associational rights implied by that status. When it acted in the delivery of public services, it was acting as a public corporation. As the concept of two types of corporations expanded, the notion of local government as private corporation became more limited. As its role as private corporation diminished, local government became seen mostly as a public corporation. However, as a public corporation, it became more regulated by the state.

By the middle of the 19th century, this new relationship of municipality as public corporation was ready to be formally introduced into American law. It was done, not through legislative action, but through judicial interpretation. This formal doctrine, often cited as Dillon's Rule, was formally adopted in 1868. Writing for the court, Dillon (*City of Clinton v. Cedar Rapids and Missouri River Railroad*) argued, "Municipal corporations owe their origin to, and derive their powers and rights wholly from the legislature. It breathes into them the breath of life, without which they cannot exist. As it created, so may it destroy. If it may destroy, it may abridge and control. Unless there is some constitutional limit on the right, the legislature might, by a single act, if we can suppose it of so great a folly, and so great a wrong, sweep from existence all municipal corporations of the state, and the corporations could not prevent it. We know of no limitation on this right, as the corporations are concerned. They are, so to phrase it, mere tenants at will of the legislature." (Dillon, 1911)

Historical context often proves helpful in understanding how and why certain decisions are made. The case that led to Dillon's Rule involved a railroad that needed to lay tracks down the middle of a city in order to fan the fires of westward economic expansion—a national priority. The city, on the other hand, did not want the tracks through the middle of town destroying the community—a local priority. To rule for the city would have threatened the nation-building process to which the country was deeply committed. Further, as Gere (1982) suggests, the prevailing beliefs of the day included an overarching image of objective, rational government staffed by the nation's elite, a concern that a co-mingling of public and private interests could not yield good government, a concern that private interests would dominate public interests, and a perceived need to protect the private economy from government intervention.

Hence, the official relationship, as articulated in Dillon's Rule, was necessary at a legal level.

However, at a practical level, American local governments have retained their private corporate status as associations. Regardless of public or private status, as corporations, the creation of a local government can be viewed both as bottom-up and an act of self-government. Although an oversimplification, it is people who create a local government, not the state government. Liberal incorporation laws in most states allow groups of citizens to make this declaration of self-government through the incorporation process.

In addition to easy incorporation statutes, some states have granted de facto corporate status to their local governments. As a result, in a number of states, particularly in the northeast and midwest, all of the territory within the state has been incorporated. In these states, the creation of new local governments occurs when residents of one incorporated territory elect to create their own government.

Not all states have all their territory incorporated into municipal governments. In a number of states, primarily in the south and west, much of the non-developed territory is unincorporated. Those unincorporated areas are provided services through the county government. Depending on the particular state laws, when development of the unincorporated territory creates a more densely populated area, that area can become incorporated. This incorporation occurs in two primary forms. The territory can become incorporated as a separate local government or the territory may be annexed into an existing incorporated municipality.

Generally, towns do not have corporate status and lack the discretionary authority of municipalities. The most notable exception to this rule is the towns of New England. Although they are referred to as towns, they were incorporated and date back to before the American Revolution. As such, they have retained significant discretionary authority and look more like cities.

Structures of Municipal Government

American municipalities are structurally organized in literally hundreds of different ways. From size of the legislature to management of the municipality, the choice is often up to the voters in the particular municipality to decide. This authority might be subject to some state limitations, but not enough to generalize that Americans have a fundamental right to decide how they want to be governed at the local level. Although exceptions abound, there are four primary organizational designs found in municipal governments. The first is the mayor-council form and the second is the council-manager form. These two structures are the most common in municipalities of over 2,500 population. The other two forms are the commission and the town meeting. These latter two forms are perhaps more important for their historical value than as popular forms of local government today.

Mayor-Council. The extent of authority vested in the mayor varies considerably. An older variant vests relatively little executive power in the mayor and is often referred to as the weak mayor-council plan (Blair, 1986: 124). In this structure, the mayor has little if any veto power over the council and may not appoint most senior administrative posts within the municipality. Its roots are found in the early 19th-century Jacksonian ideals of citizen government and fear of the concentration of power.

Particularly in larger cities, the perceived need for strong executive leadership has served to invest some mayors with far greater executive authority. This organizational form, often referred to as a strong mayor-council plan, is characterized by a clear separation of powers. The council serves as the legislature and the mayor serves as the executive exercising full appointive powers and veto powers over legislative actions of the council.

A third variant of the mayor-council plan is the strong mayor-council with chief administrative officer plan (Blair, 1986: 127). This variant adds a chief administrative officer, appointed by the mayor, to run the day-to-day operations of the city.

Although the powers of the mayor vary considerably, all forms predominantly provide for the direct election of the mayor by the citizens.

Council-Manager. In the early part of the 20th century, American local government faced two significant challenges. The first was the need to build, quickly and economically, the public infrastructure of roads, water, and other utilities. The second was the need to address serious issues of graft, corruption, and a general inefficiency in service delivery. Within the context of those needs, there also existed a set of overarching organizational principles that were believed to be almost the equivalent of "sociological law" (Nalbandian, 1991; Stillman, 1974). Initially, it was believed that there existed a clear distinction between the making of public policy and its implementation. In one domain, elected officials ought to engage in a process of making policy through legislation. In the other domain, professional managers ought to implement and administer those policies. Secondly, it was believed that local government ought to have part of its government committed to principles of political neutrality. In the end, there really was no distinction between the "Political Party A" and the "Political Party B" snowplowing program. Lastly, there existed a belief that the path to efficient and effective operations was both a desirable goal in itself and obtainable through experts.

The organizational answer to the needs of American local government was the council-manager plan. In its simplest form, the plan establishes a small council responsible for the making of public policy. That council appoints a manager who is preferably a member of the national association of experts specifically trained in the management of local governments. This manager implements the policies of the council in an objective and politically neutral manner.

It is believed that this form of local government originated in Staunton, Virginia in 1908 (Blair, 1986: 130). The plan gained credibility and relevance for larger cities with its adoption in Dayton, Ohio in 1914 and by 1921 was employed in 121 cities. By 1940 the number of communities was around 400. The principles of the manager plan resonated well with the suburban communities of metropolitan America. It has experienced rapid expansion since WWII and is now the principal form of local government in America in communities over 2,500 in population, with 3,302 recognized communities (Hansell, 2000). Translated, 75.5 million Americans live in cities operating under the council-manager plan.

Initially, the manager plan was associated with a bundle of reforms. In addition to the notion of a professional manager, the plan was often tied to the short ballot, a process wherein the voters elected only a few but important positions in the community. The long ballot included obscure administrative positions that were unfamiliar to voters but conducive to providing patronage and favors to party loyalists in a corrupt government. A second reform was at-large elections of council. The community, as a whole, was perceived as the most important consideration for an elected official. District elections would simply interfere with his pursuit of the "what's best for the community." Finally, non-partisan elections were seen as an important step in assuring that the community was "run like a business." Non-partisan elections are those where there is no political party designation of candidates on the ballot.

Many early city managers took on their new responsibilities with missionary zeal (Stillman, 1974). Not only were they bringing management improvements to a community, they perceived themselves as reformists, enlightening the unenlightened. Although ethically committed to the particular community they were serving at the moment, their ultimate responsibility was to spread this new form of government to other communities. That legacy still exists, as most managers will serve multiple communities during their careers.

On the positive side, the council-manager plan has created a national network of professionally trained managers whose career is service to local governments in a responsible and ethical fashion.[4] The International City/County Management Association (ICMA), an association of managers in service to local governments, anchors this network. Education for this network is primarily through graduate schools of public administration and management, many of which offer master's degrees specifically focused on the management of local governments. By 1995, nearly 73 percent of managers in council-manager communities held a master's or professional degree (Hansell, 2000; 18). Regulation of the network occurs primarily through adherence to an inviolate code of ethics that the membership of ICMA places on its members. This code of ethics has become deeply rooted in those communities that have adopted the council-manager plan, and has become a standard which even non-participating communities informally adopt.

The ICMA membership originally adopted the code in 1924. It has been modified several times since then, most recently in May 1998, but still retains the original principles from its origins. Given their importance as overarching principles for the way local government in America is perceived, the 12 tenets of the ICMA Code of Ethics are presented in the accompanying box.

On the negative side, since its inception, the council-manager plan has suffered from the impractical notion that politics and administration can truly be separated. In theory, the manager is not supposed to be involved in the making of policy. In practice, managers are very much involved in the policymaking process. Nalbandian (1991) refers to the desired dichotomy between politics and administration as an important symbol that is sought after but never obtained. However, the idealized pursuit legitimizes the manager plan and guides the actions of the manager in minimizing the perceived role that the manager plays in the policymaking process.

ICMA CODE OF ETHICS

Tenet 1. Be dedicated to the concepts of effective and democratic local government by responsible elected officials and believe that professional general management is essential to the achievement of this objective.

Tenet 2. Affirm the dignity and worth of the services rendered by government and maintain a constructive, creative, and practical attitude toward local government affairs and a deep sense of social responsibility as a trusted public servant.

Tenet 3. Be dedicated to the highest ideals of honor and integrity in all public and personal relationships in order that the member may merit the respect and confidence of the elected officials, of other officials and employees, and of the public.

Tenet 4. Recognize that the chief function of local government at all times is to serve the best interests of all of the people.

Tenet 5. Submit policy proposals to elected officials; provide them with facts and advice on matters of policy as a basis for making decisions and setting community goals; and uphold and implement local government policies adopted by elected officials.

Tenet 6. Recognize that elected representatives of the people are entitled to the credit for the establishment of local government policies; responsibility for policy execution rests with the members.

Tenet 7. Refrain from all political activities which undermine public confidence in professional administrators. Refrain from participation in the election of the members of the employing legislative body.

(continued)

Tenet 8. Make it a duty continually to improve the member's professional ability and to develop the competence of associates in
the use of management techniques.

Tenet 9. Keep the community informed on local government affairs;
encourage communication between the citizens and all local
government officers; emphasize friendly and courteous service
to the public; and seek to improve the quality and image of
public service.

Tenet 10. Resist any encroachment on professional responsibilities,
believing the member should be free to carry out official policies without interference, and handle each problem without
discrimination on the basis of principle and justice.

Tenet 11. Handle all matters of personnel on the basis of merit so
that fairness and impartiality govern a member's decisions,
pertaining to appointments, pay adjustments, promotions, and
discipline.

Tenet 12. Seek no favor; believe that personal aggrandizement or
profit secured by confidential information or by misuse of public time is dishonest.

Earlier, I mentioned the legal paradox of local governments, wherein
they are mere creatures of their respective state legislatures in law, but
near-inviolate institutions in practice. The role and practice of the city
manager constitutes a second great paradox in American local government. Although theoretically removed from policymaking, managers are,
in practice, important instruments in the policymaking process.

The relative advantages and disadvantages of the mayor-council and
council-manager plans have long been debated (Lyons, 1978; Lineberry
and Fowler, 1967). These efforts at comparison are inconclusive. The
council-manager plan seems to be more responsive to pressures to control overall costs while the mayor-council plan seems to be more responsive to individual constituent demands. In the end, the decision on the
appropriate organizational approach is a local one and either plan
appears to work satisfactorily. Citizens in local communities exercise the
ultimate in evaluation in that there are processes that allow communities
to switch from one form to the other if so desired.

In addition, particularly for the mayor-council and council-manager
plans, the forms of government are becoming blurred. Some have even
suggested that the distinction may have lost relevance as a way of classi-

fying forms of local governments (Svara, 2001). A 1996 study found that in governments with either a mayor-council or council-manager plan only 4 percent were pure mayor-council cities, 18 percent were pure council-manager cities and 79 percent were adaptations of the two forms (Fredrickson, Wood and Logan, 2001: 14). The principal form of adaptation for the mayor-council form is the introduction of professional management positions within the government. Conversely, the primary adaptation in the council-manager form is the presence of a mayor who may have extensive power and authority within the government.

Commission. The commission form of municipal government is similar to the structure of counties. A small elected commission, usually five members, serves as the legislative, executive, and administrative units of local government. Each member of the commission also serves as a department head of a major unit of the local government. It is currently the least used system of municipal government in America with only 2.1 percent of communities of over 2,500 population employing it (Hansell, 2000: 19).

The commission form can be traced to the early 20th century. It was part of a reform movement that sought to apply business principles to the management of local government. Advocates believed that adapting the corporate structure, where the managers of each division would form the overall company management team, would bring efficiency and effectiveness to municipal government. In addition, the direct election of department heads would keep government close and responsive to the citizens. The plan received national attention when it was adopted in Galveston, Texas in the early 1900s following a devastating hurricane. An unusually gifted and energetic set of commissioners was instrumental in rebuilding Galveston, such that the commission system was heralded as an alternative way to organize local government (Blair, 1986: 129).

Although a number of communities did adopt the commission form of government, inherent weaknesses have limited its broad adoption. The absence of executive leadership invested in one person has often resulted in a government that lacks direction. The absence of technical knowledge and professional training in the field that a commissioner directs often leads to inefficient and ineffective service delivery. Finally, accountability to the voters often becomes difficult to see as decisionmaking is diffused in a board rather than concentrated on the individuals that constitute the department heads.

When these weaknesses are combined with the popularity of the previous two forms of government, its limited use seems justified. Since

1984, the number of communities with the commission form of government has fallen by 19 percent (Hansell, 2000: 19).

Town-meeting.   The final form of local government might arguably be the
oldest and most revered. It is called the town meeting form of government and is highlighted by the legislative body that is constituted by the
citizens. Simply put, when legislative action is required, such as the
approval of an annual budget, an assembly of the citizens is called. Those
citizens who attend the meeting act as the legislature and pass laws.
Those citizens also elect a board of selectmen to serve as the administrators of the town between the town meetings. Of communities over 2,500
in population, 399 or 5.9 percent currently utilize this form of government (Hansell, 2000: 19). Like the commission form, current utilization is
on the decline. In 1984, 451 governments in the United States utilized the
town meeting form of government.

   Although the town meeting form of government is present only in
New England, and even there, in relatively few communities, its impact
on the design and structure of metropolitan organization is significant. At
a symbolic and popular level, it captures an idealized notion of citizen
government. Its impact on the American perception of governing is captured by James Bryce (1922: 591), whose treatise on the structure of government in America has informed generations of politicians, judges,
scholars and educators, when he said, "Of the three or four types of systems of local government which I have described, that of the town or
township with its primary assembly is admittedly best. It is the cheapest
and the most efficient; it is the most educative of the citizens who bear a
part in it. The town meeting has been not only the source but the school
of democracy." Because of its powerful hold on the sentiment of public
opinion, let us explore the historical roots of this institution in more
detail.

   New England communities of the 17th and 18th centuries were primarily religious institutions. As a result, the secular institutions of government emerged from the governance system of the church. One of the
cultural values that dominated these communities was a belief in the
development of consensus in the decision-making process. Where conflict, coalition building, and majority rule today are viewed as healthy
signs of an adversarial representative democracy (Mansbridge, 1980),
their presence in an 18th century New England town was viewed as a
failure of the system (Zuckerman, 1970). Rather, public values converged

on a common definition of decorum and a belief in the illegitimacy of conflict and dissent.

In these communities, the search for an appropriate public policy required unanimity and not a simple majority. However, unanimity was derived consensually. As Zuckerman (1970: 124) observes, "Even in the heat of local battles, the villagers remembered and responded to values of concord and consensus. They accommodated differences to oblige the disgruntled, separated adversaries who seemed irreconcilable, or submitted disagreements to outside arbitration; they did not drive desperately for conquest of foes, nor did they even derive any evident delight of the contest itself." In this setting, a simple majority would have carried little value and, indeed, may not have certified a decision as legitimate.

This search for consensus was possible because an ethno-religious homogeneity of citizens was able to minimize the issues that would separate the community. Secondly, a disgruntled minority would often resolve its differences with the majority by simply creating a new community where that minority became the majority. Indeed, much of the growth of New England occurred through the creation of new communities, each one looking for its version of a good society.

Within each community, inhabitants exercised a public freedom with an egalitarian spirit that seems incomprehensible from our modern-day pluralistic perspective. It was within those 18th century towns that America would approach what Arendt (1961) refers to as the Greek concept of *isonomy*—a form of government where there is no distinction between the rulers and the ruled. They practiced the art and craft of ruling and being ruled, not as a citizen who has volunteered to participate in the political arena, but as a practical matter of everyday life. The search for unanimity directed the resources and efforts of the whole community in such a manner that the rights of the minority were to be protected— not as a matter of law, but as a matter of community.

To accomplish a mutual consent of neighbors, communities sought strategies that would include all members of the town in the decision-making process. As Zuckerman (1970: 190–191) comments, "In communities in which effective enforcement depended on the moral bindingness of decisions on the men who made them, it was essential that most men be parties to such decisions." This search for inclusiveness as a means of social control was to lead to an egalitarian, direct democracy wherein the individual was free—free by virtue of his rights and obligations to participate in the decisions that affected his social world. The sovereignty of the individual was not the pursuit of private interests but the search for public consensus.

It was this system that Tocqueville (1953) observed in 1840 when he suggested, "Every individual possesses an equal share of power, and participates alike in the government of the state. He obeys the government not because he is inferior to the authorities which conduct it, or that he is less capable than his neighbor of governing himself, but because he acknowledges the utility of an association with his fellowmen, and because he knows that no such an association can exist without a regulating force."

This consensus building and search for unanimity was legitimated in the town meeting—this annual assembly of all citizens to make the laws that would govern them. The role of the town meeting was threefold. Initially, it served the purpose of affording all elements of the community a voice and a stake in determining public policy. As Zuckerman (1970: 196) notes, "Only by their participation [in town meetings] did they bind themselves to concur in the community's course of action. The town meeting was an instrument for enforcement, not a school of democracy." In the absence of a formal central authority, getting citizens to abide by decisions was often as hard as making the decision in the first place. Second, it reaffirmed the egalitarian and isonomic state of intra-community affairs. Participants exercised their capacity to rule by determining the laws by which they would be ruled and by selecting the agents who would administer the affairs of state until the next town meeting. This process reduced the social distance between top and bottom and inhibited the formation of an even more powerful oligarchic and differentiated elite than that which was formed in 18th century New England. Third, the town meeting was a ritual by which the very sense of community was continually re-established or subtly refocused.

In light of the broader purposes of the town meeting, it is understandable why these meetings were conducted with a marked absence of conflict and debate. Zuckerman (1970: 100) observes, "Resolutions were generally arranged, or at least ratified at town meetings, but they did not really originate there." Rather, "The reality of local politics rested in a hundred humble conversations, across fences and taverns, quietly allusive, subtly suggestive, endlessly tactful. If all went well, an almost silently shared understanding would be reached among the inhabitants, and there would be no contest at all for the office or issue; more often than not, the 'sense of the meeting' would be set before the meeting met" (Zuckerman 1970: 182).

The effect of the town meeting form of government has been to create a "meaning of local government utterly unlike the meaning of local government in the mother country. In England, the institutions of town and county and village reinforced the authority of the King and Parliament, thereby enhancing the tie between the people and the central government. In America, local government contributed almost nothing to the ties between the people and the central power" (Zuckerman, 1970: 228).

As suggested earlier, this form of government still exists. It has evolved over time and some communities have made significant changes (Zimmerman, 1983; Blair, 1986). One such reform is the *representative town meeting* wherein voters in larger communities elect town meeting members, usually from wards to guarantee equal representation of all parts of the community. In these communities, membership in the town meeting is usually between 120 and 270 members. A second reform is the sharing of legislative authority between the town meeting and the board of selectmen. The board is usually granted law-making authority in specific areas or can make laws subject to a fixed period of time wherein a town meeting could be called if requested. The first circumstance has given rise to the *financial town meeting* in which a town meeting passes the annual town budget. The third reform has been the introduction of the manager plan to provide executive leadership and coordination of administrative activities for the town. The manager plan works well with the town meeting form of government. The code of ethics of the manager plan resonates with the principles of openness and inclusion of town meetings and the town meeting's search for consensus allows for ease of implementation in a rational manner. For instance, of Maine's 495 communities, most of them below 2,500 in population, 156 employ the manager plan.

Although the application of the town meeting form of government is very restricted, particularly in heterogenous societies, a 1984 assessment of it as a form of government concluded, "Local lawmaking appears to be functioning adequately in most open-meeting towns in New England, and no evidence has been presented that alternative lawmakers would exercise sagacity in choosing solutions to town problems" (Zimmerman, 1984: 106).

Special/School District Government

Districts, as local government institutions, fall into two broad categories—special and school. Let us first focus on non-educational special district governments.

Special Districts

The expression "herding cats" is often used to describe a situation where the pieces of the puzzle defy categorization or ability to manage. Special districts fall into both of those categories and are, indeed, like "herding cats." Nonetheless, there are a few general observations that can be made about them. First, they represent the largest group of local governments, with 34,683 such districts in 1997. Second, they account for 90 percent of the growth in total new local governments between 1952 and 1997. Third, they tend to be single-purpose. In 1997, 92 percent of special district governments were undertaking a specific function or responsibility. Fourth, their formation usually arises from the perceived need of participants to solve a particular problem rather than as the result of a desire to address a set of complex and interrelated problems or issues in a metropolitan area.

There are two broad types of special districts. The first is generally designed to have a service territory approximately coterminous with a particular city or town government or a part of that single jurisdiction. Occasionally, that service area takes in parts of several communities. These special districts function as extensions of individual communities acting in a capacity that is isolated from the broader region of which they are a part. The second type of special district reflects a more regionalized perspective. For instance, a county government may establish a special district to serve all of the county territory or a significant percentage of the municipalities within the county. A second example is when a number of municipalities, initiated either through official action of their governments or through interested parties in those jurisdictions, create a special district to serve the needs of the municipalities, collectively. This latter form of special district will be treated in more detail in chapter 7.

Bollens (1957) and Blair (1986), among others, have analyzed why the American system accommodates and allows for the proliferation of special district governments. Initially, there is often a mismatch between the area that desires or needs a particular service and the existing political boundaries of the general-purpose governments in the area. The notion that the boundaries of the whole community would be changed to accommodate a need for a particular service is usually an unacceptable option. Secondly, there is often an inability on the part of the existing general-purpose local government to have either the power or the financial capacity to undertake a desired service. Closely associated with the lack of power and financial capacity is the lack of a willingness or administrative capacity on the part of the existing general-purpose government. For instance, a rural dominated town government may have no interest in a public water system for its urban area, even though a portion of the citizenry have such an interest. Indeed, such a situation leads to the fourth explanation. The group of citizens interested in the service being delivered may also desire control over the governance of the delivery system. The creation of the special district serves the purpose and interest of both the existing general-purpose government and the citizens that desire a service. In a situation where the common interests of government and citizen are served, it is frequently the case that the local government itself acts as the advocate for the creation of the special district. General-purpose governments, not wanting to appear to be expanding government services, particularly to voters who will not receive the service, can encourage special district formation to satisfy those citizens who want a service without alienating those citizens who fear the cost of the service might be borne by them. A sixth explanation, particularly in rural areas, centers on the desire of citizens to have some public services, but not to the degree that a general-purpose local government is required. A seventh explanation, offered by Bollens (1957: 15), is the "unadorned self-interest or selfishness of some groups and individuals." This notion of self-interest is more fully articulated in Burns (1994). She argues that a number of general-purpose and single purpose governments are formed as a direct result of business interests. Whether to produce a more favorable tax climate, a more consistent cash flow, or a better defining of the market, it is the interests of businesses and not necessarily the political interests of the citizens of the territory that are furthered. Burns demonstrates that the business interests, operating behind the scenes, often provide the financial and legal support necessary for citizens to create a new special district government.

The above explanations are derived primarily from the work of Bollens (1957). Blair (1986) adds several more explanations. The first is a "psychological attraction" in that the special district matches a tax or fee with a service in a well-defined area in a parsimonious manner that resonates well with the citizens' sense of right and appropriate behavior. Special districts are also often associated with a desire to professionalize the management of the service and appeal to a citizen's sense that the service should be delivered in an efficient and business-like manner. Finally, special districts can sometimes be used as a tool to avoid annexation to a larger city.

The picture that is painted above is one where the special district operates as an independent unit of government. Let me add a second perspective—the special district as wholly owned subsidiary of the parent government. There are two circumstances in which a government would want to create another corporation (special district) to finance or operate a service. The first is when the government needs a financing mechanism for a service without having the capital cost become part of the debt of the general government. Often referred to as a financing authority, the government creates the special district to serve as its financing arm. As an example, the City of Pittsburgh created the "Pittsburgh Water and Sewer Authority" to issue debt to finance capital improvements to the water storage and distribution system. In municipal finance, two broad types of debt can be issued to fund such infrastructure improvements. The first type is referred to as "full faith and credit" debt and means that the bonds are backed by the underlying value of all the real estate in the governmental jurisdiction. The second type is referred to as "revenue bonds." Rather than the total value of taxpayer real estate serving as collateral, the revenue stream from the ratepayers backs the bonds. Revenue bonds are generally more speculative than "full faith and credit" and were selected as the debt instrument for the improvements. Creating a separate district removes the debt financing from the books of the city.

The second circumstance occurs when it is desirable to have the operating expenses removed from the direct operation of the city. In the above case of the Pittsburgh Water and Sewer Authority, the need for rate increases to cover the capital and operating costs was, politically, difficult to do as long as those increases had to be approved by City Council. The financing authority was subsequently converted into an operating authority.

Such a move meant that a separate board, insulating both the city council and the mayor from direct political fallout, now would make decisions about rate increases. The authority, at an operational level, continued to be treated as a department of city government. Indeed, departmental meetings of the city include department heads and executive directors of several authorities.

Such a relationship is possible through the selection process of the authority. In the case of the Pittsburgh Water and Sewer Authority, the board was appointed by the mayor and included several department heads of city government. Although, under law, board members have a fiduciary responsibility to the authority, significant leeway exists, such that the interests of the city are protected along with the interests of the authority.

As a general rule, the more a single government unilaterally controls selection of the board, the more likely that authority will act as a wholly owned subsidiary of the parent government. Conversely, the less involvement of a single government in the selection process, the more the authority acts as a separate and independent government. At the other end of the continuum, many special districts directly elect the governing board.

There are two other methods of board selection that should be noted (Blair, 1986: 152). These methods generally are used when the district involves a number of municipalities directly or its coverage area encompasses a number of municipalities. *Ex officio* members, who are on the board by virtue of their current positions, may constitute board membership. For instance, public works directors of participating municipalities may serve as the board for a special district that serves those municipalities. A second method is for each participating municipality to elect a member to the board. For instance, each participating municipality may elect one of its council members to serve as a board member on the special district.

A cautionary note on the wholly owned subsidiary should be mentioned. Special districts are corporations vested with powers derived from that incorporation, which obligates a board member to protect the interests of that corporation. As a result, the wholly owned subsidiary may, over time, drift away from the parent government.

Any overall assessment of special districts in the United States context should include the issue of whether such institutions create a democracy gap. Clearly, in the case of the wholly owned subsidiary, the expectation is that the special district would continue to operate as a department of the city. Democratic principles of citizen involvement in government are not the major objective of such a formation. Instances where special districts are constituted by *ex officio* members or members elected from the existing local governments are only marginally better. The special districts may be responsive to other democratically created institutions, but they do not significantly enhance citizen engagement. Accountability of board members is only partially related to service on that particular board.

Many elected boards face the serious problem of finding a sufficient number of candidates to create competition for board membership. Secondly, voter turnout tends to be significantly less than with general government elections, with instances of less than 5 percent not unusual (Burns, 1994: 12). Given overlapping jurisdictions, multiplicity of districts, and lack of clarity of where boundaries exist, voters are often confused and frustrated in knowing whether or where they should be voting or in understanding the issues surrounding a particular special district.

Balanced against the issues surrounding the democracy gap of special districts are the utilitarian values that are served by the creation of special districts. They are, as Bollens (1957: 15) suggests, a "mixed blessing." On one hand, they are a practical response to delivering specialized services to a relevant community. On the other hand, they are not necessarily enhancing general accountability to the citizens.

School Districts

Interestingly, the highest expense category of local governments is education; yet, the discussion of school districts constitutes a relatively small part of most textbooks on the subject of local government. Most school districts are independent local governments. Of 15,834 school districts, 14,422 or 91% percent exist with an elected board and taxing powers. Of the dependent school districts, the majority are departments within a municipal government. These school departments are concentrated in the New England states of Connecticut, Maine, Massachusetts, and Rhode Island.

The reasons for this light treatment are not obvious, but several can be offered. Initially, the management form and structure of independent school districts is comparatively uniform across the United States. That form consists of a generally small (five to eleven member elected board) that serves the legislative function and a school superintendent who serves the executive function. Superintendents are selected on the basis of professional training and background in school management. A loose comparison would be to view the organization of school districts as if all municipal governments had adopted the manager plan as their organizational design.

Secondly, although education policy and management is a highly complex field, the issues in school policy are not as divergent as with municipal or county governments. Further, they tend to be focused on the internal management of the schools.

Activities of Counties and Municipalities

I have reserved the discussion of the activities engaged in by local government until the end of this chapter. Although there is a set of core activities specific to local governments, there is an extraordinarily wide range of activities, such that exceptions to the rule are commonplace. Table 3.2 presents an overview of activities engaged in by counties, cities, and townships. In addition to the activities undertaken by these units, I have also dealt with the issue of how those governments go about delivering a particular service. Governments can choose between providing the service directly or contracting with another agency or business.

The most commonly provided activities of local governments is the care and maintenance of streets. As shown in Table 3.2, 77.5 percent of all counties, 65.3 percent of all cities, and 46.3 percent of all townships assume a responsibility for streets. How that service is provided varies significantly by type of government. County governments are much more likely to deliver the service directly. For every one county government that contracts out the service there are 107.2 county governments that deliver streets services directly. Indeed, the provision of streets services is a defining service for county governments. Although city and township governments are more likely to deliver streets services directly, the frequency of contracting out is significantly higher, particularly for townships.

The emergence of county governments as deliverers of regional services is an interesting development that will be discussed in more detail later. County governments are far more likely to deliver library, solid waste, ambulance, and airport services than either city or township governments. In addition, human service activities like nursing homes and hospitals, although not typical services of county governments, are the almost-exclusive domain of county governments. Whereas less than 1 percent of city and township governments are likely to provide for nursing homes, 14.4 percent of county governments provide for that service. A similar pattern is noted for hospitals.

To assist in assessing the number of services a typical type of local government delivers, I have developed an index that I call "service density" (see Table 3.2). This index measures the number of services undertaken by a particular government. Few governments provide all twelve services identified in Table 3.2, but all governments provide at least one of the services. Based on this index, city governments provide the greatest

Table 3.2   Typical Service Functions by Type of Government, 1992

	Counties		City		Township	
	Provide %	*Direct*	*Provide %*	*Direct*	*Provide %*	*Direct*
Streets	77.5	107.2	65.3	11.0	46.3	4.8
Fire	21.1	5.8	56.6	12.9	22.0	1.7
Solid Waste	45.9	4.4	26.3	2.2	11.1	2.3
Water	11.1	7.8	65.9	26.1	5.7	6.4
Sewerage	10.6	9.2	60.5	19.5	8.4	6.4
Libraries	37.3	8.5	24.0	9.1	8.4	6.6
Ambulance	26.6	3.7	13.4	6.9	6.2	2.5
Airports	18.9	2.5	7.8	2.9	0.5	1.9
Other Utility	6.7	2.5	13.5	2.9	0.8	0.8
Nursing Homes	14.4	3.4	0.9	2.1	0.2	1.1
Hospitals	12.9	1.6	1.1	1.3	0.2	1.1
Stadiums	5.0	6.6	3.4	7.6	0.3	4.0
Service Density	2.90		3.80		1.90	

SOURCE: *U.S. Department of Commerce, Bureau of Census; Census of Governments. 1992. Volume 1: Governmental Organization.*

array of services. Of the 12 services identified in Table 3.2, City governments average 3.8 services. Streets, water, sewerage, and fire are provided by at least 56.6 percent of all city governments. The Census of Governments report from which this information was derived does not include the provision of police services. Arguably, police services are perhaps the most common of all services delivered by general-purpose local governments in the United States.

Township governments provide the least array of services and are far more likely to contract out service delivery than either city or county governments. Whereas close to 99 percent of county governments are likely to deliver streets services directly, over 20 percent of township governments are likely to contract out streets services. On average, township governments deliver half the services of city governments and approximately a third less than county governments.

Activities engaged in by special districts are presented in Table 3.3. Also noted in Table 3.3 are the changes, over time, in the purposes for which special districts serve.

Of 34,683 special districts in the United States, 31,965 (92%) are single purpose. Between 1967 and 1992 the number of such special districts grew by 53.6 percent. Only the eight services most widely delivered

Table 3.3   Types of Special Districts

	1952	1967	1987	1997	*Change %* *92/67*
School Districts	67,355	21,782	14,721	13,726	(37.0)
Special Districts	12,340	21,264	29,532	34,683	63.1
Single Purpose Districts	—	*20,811*	*27,481*	*31,965*	*53.6*
Fire Protection	2,272	3,665	5,070	5,601	52.8
Housing, Community Development	863	1,565	3,464	3,469	121.7
Water Supply	—	2,140	3,060	3,409	59.3
Drainage, Flood Control	2,380	2,855	2,772	3,369	18.0
Soil & Water Conservation	1,981	2,571	2,469	2,449	(4.7)
Sewage	429	1,233	1,607	2,004	62.5
Cemetaries	911	1,397	1,627	1,655	18.5
Libraries	269	410	830	1,496	264.9
Multi Purpose Districts	—	*453*	*2,051*	*2,718*	*500.0*
Sewerage and Water	—	298	1,168	1,384	364.4
Natural resources & water	–	45	98	117	160.0
Other[a]	83	110	785	1,217	1006.4

[a]includes fire protection and water supply and other multiple functions

Source: *U.S. Department of Commerce, Bureau of Census; Census of Governments. Volume 1: Governmental Organization. 1997, 1987.*

through special districts are presented in Table 3.3. The number one service for which a special district is utilized is fire protection. Over 5,600 such districts exist in the United States. Fire service is sensitive to a quick response in order to suppress a fire. As a result, it is a localized service that is almost universally required. As pockets of development occur, those communities move quickly to make sure that fire services are provided. Indeed, the need to provide for fire protection often precedes a perceived need by that local community to seek more broad local government powers.

Utility and infrastructure needs constitute an area in which special districts are commonly used. Water supply, drainage and flood control, soil and water conservation, and sewerage make up about a third of all special districts. These services tend not to track well with local government boundaries, such that specialized service areas provide an attractive alternative to the utilization of municipal boundaries.

The fastest growing single purpose special districts provide services in the areas of libraries and housing/community development. The number of special districts providing library services increased 264.9 percent between 1992 and 1967. Perhaps paralleling the decline in the number of school districts, libraries need to be large enough that book collections and related services serve the public economically and efficiently. The growth of housing/community development special districts was more predominant between 1967 and 1987. It was during this period that a large number of communities started experiencing the aging of the infrastructure and housing stock at the same time the federal government was both increasing funding in this area and decentralizing the funding stream away from the largest cities.

There is a second type of special district that serves more than one function. These multipurpose districts are the fastest-growing type of special district in the United States. Between 1967 and 1992, such districts grew by 500 percent. Over half of such districts provide sewerage and water services. They will be discussed in more detail later.

Notes

1. In addition to the more formal political jurisdictions, there are an additional 130,000 residential community associations (RCAs) that are "private" governments (Kincaid, 1997). These governments, from small residential subdivisions to large, planned communities like Reston, Virginia (pop. 68,000) and Columbia, Maryland (pop. 68,000), provide many government functions, and are emerging as important institutional structures in the governmental mosaic. See also: McKenzie (1994) for an in-depth treatment of RCAs.

2. The term sheriff is derived from the English "shire reeve," who was the King's appointee at the local level to collect taxes and administer royal law locally.

3. There are two primary factors that are considered in assessing whether a position meets the requirements of a single executive. The first is that the position exercises considerable power in developing the budget and financial plans of the jurisdiction. The second is that the position exercises considerable authority in the hiring process, particularly for senior management openings.

4. The rise of specially trained professionals in service to local governments extends beyond, but has been heavily influenced by, the city manager plan. Wirt (1985: 103) refers to these professional networks as "national institutions" that include "school superintendents, city managers or chief administrative officers, planning directors, city attorneys, and heads of police, fire, engineering, medical, and welfare services." The ethical and professional standards of each of these professions have become institutionalized across the United States and "impose correct ways of solving problems and doing things" on all local governments (Mosher, 1982: 118).

4

Metropolitan Regions in the United States

The world in which most local governments operate is the metropolitan region. Unfortunately, our knowledge and definition of those regions is neither uniform nor extensive. This chapter will provide as much clarity as possible. After defining what metropolitan regions are, we will look at how their organization structure differs by regions within the United States and by the population size of the metropolitan regions.

Definition of Metropolitan Regions

Local governments are political entities; metropolitan regions are not. Hence, the definition and meaning of a region becomes an artifact in the mind of the beholder. Recognizing the difficulty of standardizing a common meaning for discussion purposes, the federal government has developed a set of definitions and terminology that can serve as a starting point. It is interesting to note that originally the federal government, in defining these regions, used the term "statistical." The selection of this term was a conscious effort to establish that the nature of the boundaries was for data collection purposes only. The Federal Office of Management and Budget (OMB) is very explicit in capturing this perspective:

> MAs (metropolitan areas) are a Federal statistical standard designed solely for the preparation, presentation, and comparison of data. Before the MA (metropolitan area) concept was introduced in 1949 with Standard Metropolitan Areas (SMAs), inconsistencies between statistical area boundaries and units made comparisons of data from Federal agencies difficult.

Thus, MAs are defined according to specific, quantitative criteria (standards) to help government agencies, researchers, and others achieve uniform use and comparability of data on a national scale.

OMB recognizes that some Federal and state agencies are required by statute to use MAs for allocating program funds, setting program standards, and implementing other aspects of their programs. In defining MAs, however, OMB does not take into account or attempt to anticipate any of these non-statistical uses that may be made of MAs or their associated data. Agencies that elect to use MAs for such non-statistical purposes are advised that the standards are designed for statistical purposes only and that any changes to the standards may affect the implementation of programs (OMB Bulletin 99–04).

However, over time, these regions have come to take on more than a data collection role. More often than not, individuals, groups, and organizations in these regions are beginning to think of themselves as citizens of the region. Federal policy has encouraged the formation of embryonic regional institutions around those boundaries. As a result, we can, on a limited basis, see these regions as political as well as data collection entities. Indeed, the transformation of metropolitan regions from artificial data collection areas to political bodies is not unlike the transformation of county government over the last two centuries. In addition, the federal government has used a definition of common interrelationship and interdependency to draw the boundaries on these metropolitan areas. As such, these metropolitan regions are perhaps, unwittingly, anticipating the future of urban America.

The Federal Office of Management and Budget (OMB) categorizes regions based on three designations: metropolitan statistical areas (MSA), consolidated metropolitan statistical areas (CMSA), and primary metropolitan statistical areas (PMSA). Another way to think about these definitions is as follows: MSAs are stand-alone regions and CMSAs are megaregions that are made up of collections of MSAs. When an MSA is part of a mega-region, it is simply referred to as a PMSA. Common to all is the notion of a core area containing a large population nucleus, together with adjacent communities that are economically and socially integrated with that core. These regions are grouped on the basis of county boundaries. Proving that even these larger groupings are subject to exceptions to the rule, cities and towns in New England are the geographic building blocks of the regions.

The system works as follows. Any area in the United States that has one city with at least a population of 50,000 is defined by the Census Bureau as an urbanized area (which means there is a definable urbanized area of at least a population of 50,000) and a total population of 100,000 as a metropolitan area (MA). For naming purposes, the county (or counties) that contains the largest city becomes the "central county." In New England, that designation is made based on the largest cities and towns.

How large the metropolitan area will be is defined by the relationship of outlying counties to the center. Generally, commuter patterns, density requirements and high growth are standards that are used to create the link between the outlying areas with the center. These criteria demonstrate that interdependency exists such that the area shares a common future. An outlying county will be included in an MSA if any one of the following conditions is met:

At least 50 percent of the employed workers residing in the county commute to the core, *and* either the population density of the county is at least 25 persons per square mile, or at least 10 percent, or at least 5,000 of the population lives in an urbanized area;

From 40 to 50 percent of the employed workers commute to the central county/counties, *and* either the population density is at least 35 persons per square mile, or at least 10 percent, or at least 5,000, of the population lives in an urbanized area;

From 25 to 40 percent of the employed workers commute to the central county/counties *and* either the population density of the county is at least 50 persons per square mile, *or any two* of the following conditions exist: population density is at least 35 persons per square mile; at least 35 percent of the population is urban; and, at least 10 percent, or at least 5,000 of the population lives in an urbanized area;

From 15 to 25 percent of the employed workers commute to the central county/counties and the population density of the county is at least 50 persons per square mile, *and any two* of the following conditions also exist: population density is at least 60 persons per square mile; at least 35 percent of the population is urban; population growth between the last two decennial censuses is at least 20 percent; at least 10 percent, or at least 5,000, of the population lives in an urbanized area;

From 15 to 25 percent of the employed workers commute to the central county/counties and the population density of the county is less than 50 persons per square mile, *and any two* of the following conditions also exist: at least 35 percent of the population is urban; population growth between the last two decennial censuses is at least 20 percent; at least 10 percent, or at least 5,000, of the population lives in an urbanized area;

At least 2,500 of the population live in a central city of the MSA located in an urbanized area.

As of the June 30, 1999, there are 258 MSAs and 18 CMSAs comprising 73 PMSAs in the United States. In addition, there were 3 MSAs, 1 CMSA, and 3 PMSAs in Puerto Rico. Naming the regions is done in an objective fashion. Up to three of the largest cities in each MSA and CMSA are designated a "central city or cities." Titles of PMSAs also typically are based on central city names but in certain cases consist of county names. Generally, titles of CMSAs are based on the titles of their component PMSAs.

The eighteen mega-regions (CMSA) and their constituent regions (PMSA) are listed in Table 4.1. Only two of these mega-regions are made up of more than six regions. The New York CMSA is made up of 15 regions in the states of New York, Connecticut, New Jersey. The Boston CMSA is made up of 10 regions in the states of Massachusetts and New Hampshire. Other mega-regions cross state boundaries. The Philadelphia CMSA spans three states; Pennsylvania, and New Jersey, and Delaware. The Chicago CMSA covers parts of Illinois and Wisconsin.

On a population basis, the 18 CMSAs are joined with 8 MSAs to form the largest of the metropolitan regions. Slightly less than 47 percent of the total United States population lives in these 26 regions. Few of these regions significantly changed their population rank between 1990 and 1999 (see Table 4.2). Atlanta (from 13th to 11th), Phoenix (from 19th to 14th) and Denver (21st to 19th) grew enough to change more than two ranks. On the population loss side, Pittsburgh (18th to 20th) and Milwaukee (24th to 26th) dropped two or more ranks during that same period.

Variation in Metropolitan Regions

I want to turn to a discussion of how these metropolitan regions are structurally organized. That structure can be assessed and contrasted based on the overall size of the metropolitan region as well as the part of the United States in which the metropolitan region is located. Generally, we have used the term "region" to mean a metropolitan area made up of a number of local governments. Another use of the term "region" is in reference to a particular part of the United States. In this context, states have been grouped together in what are considered regions of the United

Table 4.1   The Eighteen Consolidated Metropolitan Statistical Areas
(CMSAs)in the United States

CMSA or Mega-Regions	Region of USA	Metropolitan Area (PMSAs) s within the CMSA
Boston, MA	Northeast	(10) Boston, MA; Brockton, MA; Fitchburg, MA; Lawrence, MA; Manchester, NH; Nashua, NH; New Bedford, MA; Portsmouth, NH; Worcester, MA
Chicago, IL	Midwest	(4) Chicago, IL; Gary, IN; Kankakee, IL; Kenosha, WI
Cincinnati, OH	Midwest	(2) Cincinnati, OH; Hamilton, OH
Cleveland, OH	Midwest	(2) Akron, OH; Cleveland; OH
Dallas, TX	South	(2) Dallas, TX; Fort Worth, TX
Denver, CO	West	(3) Boulder, CO; Denver, CO; Greeley, CO
Detroit, MI	Midwest	(3) Ann Arbor, MI; Detroit, MI; Flint, MI
Houston, TX	South	(3) Brazoria, TX; Galveston, TX; Houston, TX
Los Angeles, CA	West	(4) Los Angeles, CA; Orange County, CA; Riverside, CA; Ventura County, CA
Miami, FL	South	(2) Fort Lauderdale, FL; Miami, FL
Milwaukee, WI	Midwest	(2) Milwaukee, WI; Racine, WI
New York, NY	Northeast	(15) Bergen, NJ; Bridgeport, CT; Danbury, CT; Dutchess County, NY; Jersey City, NJ; Middlesex, NJ; Monmouth, NJ; Nassau, NY; New Haven, CT; New York City, NY; Newark, NJ; Newburgh, NY; Stamford, CT; Trenton, NJ; Waterbury, CT
Philadelphia, PA	Northeast	(4) Atlantic City, NJ; Philadelphia, PA; Vineland, NJ; Wilmington, DE
Portland, OR	West	(2) Portland, OR; Salem, OR
Sacramento, CA	West	(2) Sacramento, CA; Yolo, CA
San Francisco, CA	West	(6) Oakland, CA; San Francisco, CA: San Jose, CA; Santa Cruz, CA; Santa Rose, CA; Vallejo, CA
Seattle, WA	West	(4) Bremerton, WA; Olympia, WA: Seattle, WA; Tacoma, WA
Washington, DC	South	(3) Baltimore, MD; Hagerstown, MD; Washington, DC

SOURCE: *http://www.bureauofcensus.gov*

States. These "regions of states" are important in explaining variance in how metropolitan regions are managed. The "regions of states" are defined by the Census Bureau and grouped into the northeast, midwest, south and west.

Metropolitan regions, including both MSAs and PMSAs, have also been grouped into five categories based on their population size. Those groupings are: "Large": over 2,000,000; "Medium Large": 1,000,000 to

Table 4.2   Population Change for the Largest Metropolitan Regions, 1990-1999

Region by Central City			Population Rank		
CMSA	MSA	Population	1999	1990	Change
New York City		20,197	1	1	
Los Angeles		16,037	2	2	
Chicago		8,886	3	3	
Washington D.C.		7,359	4	4	
San Francisco		6,874	5	5	
Philadelphia		5,999	6	6	
Boston		5,667	7	7	
Detroit		5,469	8	8	
Dallas		4,910	9	9	
Houston		4,494	10	10	
	Atlanta	3,857	11	13	p
Miami		3,711	12	11	
Seattle		3,466	13	12	
	Phoenix	3,014	14	19	p
Cleveland		2,911	15	14	
	Minneapolis	2,872	16	15	
	San Diego	2,821	17	16	
	St. Louis	2,569	18	17	
Denver		2,418	19	21	p
	Pittsburgh	2,331	20	18	q
	Tampa	2,278	21	20	
Portland		2,181	22	23	
Cincinnati		1,961	23	22	
	Kansas City	1,756	24	25	
Sacramento		1,741	25	26	
Milwaukee		1,648	26	24	q
Total of 26 Largest MSAs		127,427			
Balance of Metropolitan Areas		91,180			
Non Metro Areas		54,084			
Total Population (in 000's)		272,691			

SOURCE: *http://www.bureauofcensus.gov*

2,000,000; "Medium": 500,000 to 999,999; "Medium Small": 250,000 to 499,999; and "Small": under 250,000.

Of the 331 MSAs and PMSAs, I have collected comprehensive data on 311 regions. Table 4.3 profiles those regions. Two observations can be made about the data in the table. First, metropolitan regions are not

Table 4.3   Distribution of Regions by "Regions-of-States" and Population
Size, 1992

	Northeast		Midwest		South		West		Total	
	No.	Percent	No.	Percent	No.	Percent	No.	Percent	No.	Percent
Small	13	28.3	49	56.3	56	45.9	23	41.1	141	45.3
Medium Small	11	23.9	18	20.7	30	24.6	14	25.0	73	23.5
Medium	7	15.2	10	11.5	17	13.9	7	12.5	41	13.2
Medium Large	8	17.4	5	5.7	13	10.7	6	10.7	32	10.3
Large	7	15.2	5	5.7	6	4.9	6	10.7	24	7.7
Total	46	14.8	87	28.0	122	39.2	56	18.0	311	100.0

SOURCE: *http://www.bureauofcensus.gov*

evenly distributed throughout the "regions of states." The south holds about 40 percent of all metropolitan regions, while the northeast is home to less than 15 percent of the metropolitan regions. Second, most metropolitan regions are relatively small.[1] Overall, 45.3 percent of all metropolitan regions are under 250,000 population and close to 70 percent of all regions are under 500,000 population. Less than 8 percent of metropolitan regions are over one million population. The concentration of small regions is greatest in the midwest where 56.3 percent of metropolitan regions are under 250,000 population. Conversely, the northeast has the lowest concentration of small metropolitan regions, even though their fundamental building blocks are municipalities and not county governments.

The government structure of metropolitan regions is presented in Table 4.4. What is most striking is the high number of local governments in a typical metropolitan area. Metropolitan regions in the northeast average 169.4 local governments while metropolitan regions in the south average 57.0 local governments. The midwest looks more like the northeast with 128.9 local governments and the west looks more like the south with 103.3 local governments.

The structural complexity of metropolitan regions emerges when we consider the northeast, where a metropolitan region is made up of 2.2 county governments, 75.6 municipal governments, 58.3 special districts and 33.4 school districts. Even in the relatively structurally-concentrated south, a metropolitan area is made up of 2.7 county governments, 20.2 municipal governments, 26.3 special districts and 8.3 school districts.

In addition to the number of local governments, "regions of states" also differ on the types of local governments more commonly found. Close to

Table 4.4   Average Number of Governments in Metropolitan Regions by "Region-of-States," 1991

| | County | | Municipalities | | Districts | | | | Total | |
| | | | | | Special | | School | | | |
	#	%	#	%	#	%	#	%	#	%
Northeast	2.2	1.3%	75.6	44.6%	58.3	34.4%	33.4	19.7%	169.4	100.0%
Midwest	2.5	1.9%	64.0	49.7%	38.4	29.8%	24.0	18.6%	128.9	100.0%
South	2.7	4.7%	20.2	35.4%	26.3	46.1%	8.3	14.6%	57.0	100.0%
West	1.4	1.4%	14.8	14.3%	64.3	62.2%	22.8	22.1%	103.3	100.0%

SOURCE: *U.S. Department of Commerce, Bureau of Census*

half of all local governments in the northeast and midwest are municipalities, whereas close to 85 percent of all local governments, in a typical west metropolitan area, are either special or school districts.

Notes

1. Small is a relative term. However, one of the most comprehensive efforts to deal scientifically with the appropriate size of local governments was conducted by the British government in the early 1970s and concluded that 250,000 population was a minimum threshold size for a comprehensive local government. The structure of English local government was significantly redesigned based on that conclusion. Although I am not suggesting its appropriateness, it does suggest that a scale size of 250,000 population might well be considered "small."

5

Difference in State Systems and Metropolitan Areas

We have identified and reviewed the major institutions of local government and we have defined, as best we can, the metropolitan regions of the United States. The foundation has now been laid to deal directly with the issue of how and why there is such significant variation in local government in the United States. Although I spent a significant amount of time in the last chapter laying out the metropolitan regions, we must initially revert back to assessing this question at the state level. However, at the end of this chapter, I will return to the metropolitan region to introduce an emerging field of research specifically designed for comparative metropolitan analysis.

Nowhere in the United States Constitution does the term "local government" appear. Such an omission has been referred to as a "tragic oversight" (Mumford, 1961: 28). The term itself was probably not even used until the 19th century. A weak consensus traces the term to Jeremy Bentham around 1830 (Wickwar, 1970: 19). However, the concept of substate territorial units (townships) was well established and formed the organizational structure around which the American colonies developed and the American Revolution was fought (Arendt, 1963; Mumford, 1961).

Instead of constitutionally derived powers, the definition and purpose of local government has been left to the court system to resolve. Although the basic political question of the power relationship between a state government and the local governments within its quarters has yet to be resolved, a legal resolution can be said to have occurred in 1868. Writing for the Iowa Supreme Court, Justice Dillon[1] defined local governments as "mere tenants at will of their respective state legislatures" and limited in their performance to a narrowly defined set of public activities (*City of*

Table 5.1   Top and Bottom States in Number of Local Governments, 1997

	Square Miles	1990 Population	Total	County	Municipality		District	
					City	Town	School[a]	Special
Illinois	57,918	11,431,000	6,835	102	1,288	1,433	944	3,068
Pennsylvania	46,058	11,882,000	5,586	66	1,023	1,546	516	2,435
Texas	268,601	16,987,000	4,700	254	1,177	0	1,087	2,182
California	163,707	29,760,000	4,607	57	471	0	1,069	3,010
Kansas	82,282	2,478,000	3,950	105	627	1,370	324	1,524
Ohio	44,828	10,847,000	3,597	88	941	1,310	666	592
Minnesota	86,943	4,375,000	3,501	87	854	1,794	360	406
Missouri	69,709	5,117,000	3,416	114	944	324	537	1,497
Indiana	36,420	5,544,000	3,198	91	569	1,008	294	1,236
Wisconsin	65,503	4,892,000	3,059	72	583	1,266	442	696
New York	54,475	17,990,000	3,009	57	615	929	686	722
Arizona	114,006	3,665,000	637	15	87	0	231	304
Connecticut	5,544	3,287,000	583	0	30	149	17	387
New Hampshire	9,351	1,109,000	575	10	13	221	166	165
Virginia	42,769	6,187,000	483	95	231	0	1	156
Louisiana	51,843	4,220,000	467	60	302	0	66	39
Maryland	12,407	4,781,000	420	23	156	0	0	241
Delaware	2,489	666,000	336	3	57	0	19	257
Nevada	110,567	1,202,000	205	16	19	0	17	153
Alaska	656,424	550,000	175	12	149	0	0	14
Rhode Island	1,545	1,003,000	119	0	8	31	4	76
Hawaii	10,932	1,108,000	19	3	1	0	0	15

[a]This column reflects the number of independent school districts. School systems that are part of larger governments are not included in the total.

SOURCE: *U.S. Department of Commerce, Bureau of Census; Census of Governments, 1997. Volume 1: Governmental Organization.*

Clinton v. Cedar Rapids and Missouri River Railroad). This legal doctrine has received different interpretations, such that there currently exists a wide variation in state and local relations, ranging from extensive state involvement in local affairs to relative freedom of local elections. Indeed, the American system is actually fifty different systems of state and local government activities, functions, and responsibilities.

Although the number of governments does not necessarily reflect the presence or absence of power, it dramatizes the different approaches that have been taken by American states. Table 5.1 identifies the ten states with the most number of local governments and the ten states with the least number. A cursory review of the data suggests that geography and population size have a modest impact on a state's decision to create a few or many units of local government.

The ten states with many local governments all have at least 3,000 units. Utilization of school districts and special districts is also a common

Table 5.2   Land and Population Density of Local Governments in States
with Most and Fewest Units of Local Government

	Government Every	
	Square Miles	*Population*
Illinois	8,474	1,672
Pennsylvania	8,245	2,127
Texas	57,149	3,614
California	35,534	6,460
Kansas	20,831	627
Ohio	12,463	3,016
Minnesota	24,834	1,250
Missouri	20,407	1,498
Indiana	11,388	1,734
Wisconsin	21,413	1,599
New York	18,104	5,979
Arizona	178,973	5,754
Connecticut	9,509	5,638
New Hampshire	16,263	1,929
Virginia	88,549	12,810
Louisiana	111,013	9,036
Maryland	29,540	11,383
Delaware	7,408	1,982
Nevada	539,351	5,863
Alaska	3,750,994	3,143
Rhode Island	12,983	8,429
Hawaii	575,368	58,316

SOURCE: *U.S. Department of Commerce, 1997 Census of Governments. Volume 1: Governmental Organization.*

feature of those states. Except for Texas and California, these states generally have high instances of utilization of the town form of government and are generally located in the northeast and midwest.

The states on the other end of the continuum are far more heterogeneous. Initially, it includes the smallest state, Rhode Island, and the largest state, Alaska. It includes states from New England, the south, as well as the west, Alaska and Hawaii. Finally, it includes the first state (Delaware) to join the union as well as the last two states (Alaska and Hawaii).

Table 5.2 addresses the concentration of local governments based on the land area and population of the state. A number of states have the equivalent of a local government every 10,000 or so square miles. They fall into both categories of states with large numbers of local governments (Illinois and Pennsylvania) and states with fewer numbers of local government (Connecticut and Delaware). It is also not uncommon for there to be the equivalent of a local government for a relatively few people. In Kansas, there is a government for every 627 residents of the state. Only a few states exceed 10,000 residents per local government, with Hawaii being a true outlier with over 58,000 residents per local government.

I will use two methods to explore in greater detail the differences in systems of state and local government in United States. Initially, I will present some descriptive work that seeks to identify how the major local government institutions vary by state. Some states prefer greater utilization of county government, while other states rely heavily on special districts, and others place greater emphasis on cities and towns. I refer to this as the Stephens-Wikstrom Analysis of State Variation in Local Government Systems or the "descriptive analysis." The second approach is more explanatory and seeks to identify what characteristics of state systems seem to account for this wide variation in approaches. I refer to this as Miller's Four Dimensional Analysis of State Variation in Local Government Systems, or the "explanatory analysis."

The Descriptive Analysis

An important, systematic effort to quantify differences in systems of local governments in the United States is found in the work of Stephens and Wikstrom (1999: 126–144). They use three criteria to assess the relative role a particular type of local government plays in the overall system. The first criterion measures the size of the bureaucracy in terms of the number of employees per unit of population. The second criterion measures per capita revenues and the third measures per capita expenditures. These measures are indexed and the average state is assigned a value of 100, with all other states measured against that average value. For instance, all of the county governments in each state are aggregated to determine the size of their bureaucracy, their own source revenues, and their own source expenditures relative to all of the other county systems in all the other states. In the case of county government, the average county system is found in New Jersey and New Jersey's county government activity is assigned a score of 100. Relative to New Jersey, county governments in Maryland are approximately 3.5 times more active and received an index score of 359.4. At the other extreme, Vermont's county governments received an index score of 1.6. Compared to New Jersey, Vermont's county governments are almost nonexistent.

Table 5.3   Distribution of Powers Between Primary Forms of Local Government in the Northeast

	County	Municipal		Districts	
		City	*Township*	*Special*	*School*
Connecticut	*Neg*	**Hyp**	**Hyp**	BA	*Neg*
Maine	*Neg*	**Hyp**	**Hyp**	BA	AA
Massachusetts	*Neg*	**Hyp**	**Hyp**	AA	*Neg*
New Hampshire	Low	AA	AA	*Neg*	AA
New Jersey	A	A	**Hyp**	BA	AA
New York	BA	**Hyp**	AA	BA	BA
Pennsylvania	BA	BA	BA	AA	**Hyp**
Rhode Island	*Neg*	**Hyp**	**Hyp**	Low	*Neg*
Vermont	*Neg*	A	AA	*Neg*	**Hyp**

Key: *Neg* - Negligible; Low - Low; BA - Below Average; A - Average; AA - Above Average; **Hyp** - Hyperactive

Source: *Adapted from: Stephens, G. R. and N. Wikstrom (1999). Metropolitan government and Governance: Theoretical Perspectives, Empirical Analysis, and the Future. New York: Oxford University Press. p. 124–146*

This process of developing an index is replicated for the two types of municipal governments (cities and townships) and for special districts. Although their classification system of municipalities is slightly different than my definition, it is close enough for us to make general assumptions about variations in the states.

Stephens and Wikstrom converted their index to categories. When the particular form of local government in a state received an index score between 80 and 120 it was classified as "average." Those states where the form of local government received an index score between 120 and 150 were classified as "above average." In states where activity exceeded 150 on the index, the state was classified as "hyperactive." Conversely, states where the particular form of local government received an index score between 80 and 50 were classified as "below average." States that scored between 50 and 25 were classified as "low" and scores below 25 were classified as "negligible."

Utilizing the major regions of the United States identified in the last chapter, we can systematically review the results of their analysis. Table 5.3 looks at the states in the northeast. Broadly speaking, the most active governments in the northeast are the cities and townships. With the exception of New Hampshire, Pennsylvania, and Vermont, these states have hyperactive municipal governments. In New Hampshire and Vermont, municipal governments are above average in their relative role.

Table 5.4   Distribution of Powers Between Primary Forms of Local Government in the Midwest

| | County | Municipal | | Districts | |
		City	Township	Special	School
Illinois	BA	A	Neg	**Hyp**	AA
Indiana	A	BA	Neg	BA	AA
Iowa	A	BA		Neg	AA
Kansas	A	A	Neg	BA	AA
Kentucky	A	A		Low	A
Michigan	BA	BA	BA	Low	**Hyp**
Minnesota	A	A	Low	AA	A
Missouri	Low	A	Neg	A	AA
Nebraska	BA	BA	Neg	**Hyp**	AA
North Dakota	BA	BA	Neg	BA	**Hyp**
Ohio	A	BA	Low	BA	AA
South Dakota	BA	A	Neg	Low	**Hyp**
Wisconsin	A	BA	Low	Low	**Hyp**

Key: *Neg* - Negligible; Low - Low; BA - Below Average; A - Average; AA - Above Average; **Hyp** - Hyperactive

SOURCE: *Adapted from: Stephens, G. R. and N. Wikstrom (1999). Metropolitan Government and Governance: Theoretical Perspectives, Empirical Analysis, and the Future. New York: Oxford University Press. p. 124–146*

Only Pennsylvania has a relatively modest role for its municipal governments. In Pennsylvania and Vermont, where municipal roles are unlike the other states, the role of the school district is very prominent.

Common to all states in this region is the limited role of county government. In the New England states (Connecticut, Maine, Massachusetts, Rhode Island, Vermont), county government plays a negligible role. The role of special districts is generally limited in this region. Massachusetts and Pennsylvania are notable exceptions in that special districts play an above-average role. The absence of a school district role in Connecticut, Massachusetts, and Rhode Island generally means that the municipality has retained the responsibility for schools.

Table 5.4 assesses the midwest region of the United States. This area of the country utilizes school districts much more than in the northeast. Four of the 13 states have hyperactive school districts and another seven have school districts that play an above average role relative to all of the school districts in United States. Interestingly, except for Illinois, Minnesota and Nebraska, high utilization of school districts is not translated into high utilization of other forms of special districts.

Table 5.5 Distribution of Powers Between Primary Forms of Local Government in the South

| | County | Municipal | | Districts | |
		City	*Township*	*Special*	*School*
Alabama	BA	A		**Hyp**	A
Arkansas	BA	A		*Neg*	AA
Delaware	BA	BA		Low	AA
Florida	AA	BA		AA	A
Georgia	A	BA		**Hyp**	A
Louisiana	A	A		*Neg*	A
Maryland	**Hyp**	*Neg*		BA	*Neg*
Mississippi	AA	BA		*Neg*	AA
North Carolina	**Hyp**	BA		A	BA
Oklahoma	BA	A		*Neg*	AA
South Carolina	A	BA		A	AA
Tennessee	**Hyp**	AA		BA	*Neg*
Texas	BA	A		AA	AA
Virginia	**Hyp**	Low		BA	*Neg*
West Virginia	BA	BA		Low	**Hyp**

Key: *Neg* - Negligible; Low - Low; BA - Below Average; A - Average; AA - Above Average; **Hyp** - Hyperactive

SOURCE: *Adapted from: Stephens, G. R. and N. Wikstrom (1999). Metropolitan Government and Governance: Theoretical Perspectives, Empirical Analysis, and the Future. New York: Oxford University Press. p. 124–146*

Although township governments exist in this region, their power, unlike in the northeast, is extremely limited. City governments, although utilized in all states, play, at best, a modest role, as do county governments. It also appears that there is little trade-off between the relative role of county government and city government. In five of the states (Kansas, Kentucky, Minnesota, Nebraska, and North Dakota) the relative role of city and county government is the same. In Illinois, South Dakota, and Missouri, county government is less utilized and city government is more utilized. In the other states, the situation is reversed; lower utilization of city government corresponds to a higher utilization of county government.

Table 5.5 looks at the southern region of the United States. Common to all states in this region-of-states is the absence of the township form of government. Apart from that similarity, this region is difficult to categorize. It has the most active county governments (Maryland, North Carolina, Tennessee, and Virginia). Yet, it also has a number of states where county government's role is under-utilized. The role of city government ranges from negligible in Maryland to above average in Tennessee.

Table 5.6   Distribution of Powers Between Primary Forms of Local
Government in the West

	County	Municipal		Districts	
		City	Township	Special	School
Arizona	A	A		**Hyp**	A
California	A	A		**Hyp**	A
Colorado	BA	A		**Hyp**	AA
Idaho	A	BA		A	AA
Montana	A	BA		Low	**Hyp**
Nevada	**Hyp**	BA		BA	A
New Mexico	BA	A		*Neg*	A
Oregon	BA	BA		**Hyp**	**Hyp**
Utah	BA	BA		**Hyp**	A
Washington	BA	BA		**Hyp**	A
Wyoming	AA	BA		**Hyp**	**Hyp**

Key: *Neg* - Negligible; Low - Low; BA - Below Average; A - Average; AA - Above Average; **Hyp** - Hyperactive

SOURCE: *Adapted from: Stephens, G. R. and N. Wikstrom (1999). Metropolitan Government and Governance: Theoretical Perspectives, Empirical Analysis, and the Future. New York: Oxford University Press. pp. 124–146*

The utilization of special districts also varies widely. Negligible utilization in Arkansas, Louisiana, Mississippi, and Oklahoma is offset by hyperactive utilization in Alabama and Georgia. School district utilization follows a similar pattern; from hyperactive use in West Virginia to negligible use in Maryland, Tennessee, and Virginia, where schools are administered through the county government.

Table 5.6 focuses on the west region of the United States. Like the south, the township form of government is nonexistent. Unlike the south, this region is much more homogeneous in the distribution of power among its local government institutions. It is highlighted by the hyperactive utilization of special districts in seven of the eleven states. It is the area of the United States that relies the heaviest on special districts. The outliers are Nevada's utilization of county government and New Mexico's under-utilization of special districts.

Table 5.7 is included for purposes of completeness and includes the states of Hawaii and Alaska. It is interesting to note that in the newest states to enter the union, the county form of government (called a borough in Alaska) is the dominant form of government for both of those states.

Table 5.7   Distribution of Powers Between Primary Forms of Local Government in Alaska and Hawaii

	County	Municipal		Districts	
		City	*Township*	*Special*	*School*
Hawaii	**Hyp**	*Neg*		*Neg*	*Neg*
Alaska	**Hyp**	A		*Neg*	*Neg*

Key: *Neg* - Negligible; Low - Low; BA - Below Average; A - Average; AA - Above Average; **Hyp** - Hyperactive

SOURCE: *Adapted from: Stephens, G. R. and N. Wikstrom (1999). Metropolitan Government and Governance: Theoretical Perspectives, Empirical Analysis, and the Future. New York: Oxford University Press. pp. 124–146*

Although there are significant variations, the above analysis generally supports prior work that identifies strong municipal government in the northeast, higher utilization of county government in the south, and the powerful role of special districts in the west.

The Explanatory Analysis

To suggest that variation is purely a function of region, however, would be extremely misleading. In Figure 1.1, it was suggested that a particular state system could be seen as the interaction between four principal institutions—the citizen, local government, state government, and the federal government. There are at least four dimensions that can be used to explain differences in systems of local government in the United States. The first is a politico-legal dimension that captures how particular state legislatures have defined the role of local government within their state system. The second is a cultural dimension that reflects the values and orientation of a particular state relative to its view of the nature of civil society, the types of rules that ought to govern that society, and a general sense of who ought to participate in the making of those rules. The third is a geo-spatial dimension that reflects variation in geography, topology, population, and demographics in each of the states. The fourth is an economic dimension, reflecting that states do not have equal resources and that some states have healthier economies than others.

Returning to Figure 1.1, we could now present a graphic depiction of the four dimensions on the interaction of principal institutions. This has been

Figure 5.1   Four Explanatory Dimensions for Differences in State Systems

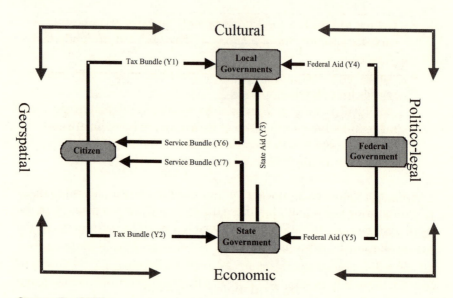

SOURCE: *David Miller*

done in Figure 5.1. Unlike the descriptive analysis, which looked at variation in types of local governments utilized, this explanatory analysis looks at local government utilization without distinction between the types of local government. Instead, it looks at total taxes raised by local governments as opposed to state governments in each state as well as the expenditure patterns of local as opposed to state government. The four dimensions, when taken together, accounted for 83 percent of the variation between states for their total state and local government tax efforts for the 1982 tax year; 82 percent of the total state and local government operating expenditures for 1982; and 45 percent of differences in state aid (Miller, 1988).

Politico-Legal Dimension

Recognizing the ability of respective state legislatures to define the role of local government within their state, the first dimension is politico-legal. One way to capture this dimension is to consider the discretionary authority vested with local governments in a particular state.

Zimmerman (1983) has operationalized discretionary authority based on four criteria. Those criteria are:

- Degree to which a local government can raise revenues necessary to support the functions it has decided to undertake (finance);
- Ability of a local government to choose activities or functions it wishes to undertake (function);
- Ability of a local government to regulate and determine the makeup and responsibilities of its workforce (personnel); and
- Degree to which a local government can define its own organizational structure (structure).

Although Zimmerman treated all four factors equally, weighting those factors is important. Such a process does carry subjectivity that reflects, to a degree, my intuitive assessment. Adequate finances and the flexibility to raise revenues are fundamental to governments. Absent the resources, all other discussions are academic. Finance, therefore, is most important. Second, the ability to select the activities that the government will engage in based on local initiative and interest constitutes the next most important element of discretionary authority. Many local governments are constrained by legislative prohibitions on the activities in which a local government can engage. Function, therefore, is second.

Next in importance is control over personnel. Several years ago, I assisted in the development of a fiscal recovery plan for the city of Scranton, Pennsylvania. The population of the city had declined from 140,000 to around 80,000 by 1990, resulting in fiscal deficits that were bankrupting the city. One area that represented significant savings to the city was a reduction in the size of the fire department. I successfully negotiated with the fire union to reduce the size of the department of 200 firefighters to 150. This process was made difficult by virtue of special legislation that had been passed by the Pennsylvania Legislature mandating that Scranton have 200 firefighters. In prior years, the union of firefighters of the city had been able to convince the state legislature to impose this standard on the government of the city.

The last criterion is structure. Structure is clearly important, but given the standardization of the council-manager plan and the mayor-council plan, most local governments in the United States have reasonable access to define the appropriate organizational structure of their government.

Zimmerman (1983) used a five-point scale ranging from one (which represented high discretion) to five (which represented little discretion) on each of the four factors. For purposes of our discussion, I have multiplied the score on finance by 4, the score on function by 3, the score on personnel by 2, and the score on structure by 1. This results in a score for each state that ranges from a minimum of 10, that would represent a high degree of local government discretionary authority, to a maximum of 50, that would represent minimal local discretionary authority. When this system is applied to the 48 contiguous states, the resulting scores range from a low of 13 in Maine and Texas to a high of 40 in New Mexico. The full listing of scores is presented in Table 5.8.

When we apply this measure of local discretionary authority to fiscal features of the intergovernmental system, a number of important observations emerge. Initially, the greater the number of units of local government in a state, the greater is the tendency for the state to grant increased discretionary authority to those units. More governments create more complexity for state officials and, as a result, local governments are afforded a greater opportunity to exercise their own initiatives.

Secondly, population serves a similar function. As states become more populated, there is a tendency toward greater local discretion. This observation is consistent with the findings of Berman and Martin (1988). However, density works in the opposite direction. As density increases, the amount of discretionary authority tends to decrease. Apparently, density works to create pressures on the state system to regulate the interplay of local government actors. Interestingly, as the variation in population density within a state increases, the resulting wide differences lead to local governments having greater discretionary authority. In states where there are both highly urbanized areas and highly rural areas, the practical implications are two very different realities—the rural and the urban—such that greater discretionary authority would be necessary to respond to those different realities.

Political Culture Dimension

A second dimension is cultural. This notion is suggested by the work of Elazar (1966, 1984) who has classified three dynamically interactive political subcultures embedded within the American society. These cultural perspectives establish frames of reference by which the debate over the role and nature of local government is processed in each state. Political

Table 5.8   Municipal Discretionary Authority Scores by State

	State	Score	State	Score	
↑	Maine	13	Delaware	25	
	Texas	13	New Hampshire	25	
	Michigan	14	Wyoming	27	
H	Connecticut	16	Florida	28	L
I	North Carolina	16	Mississippi	28	O
G	Maryland	17	Tennessee	28	W
H	Oregon	17	Arkansas	29	E
E	Illinois	18	Kentucky	29	R
R	Missouri	18	New Jersey	29	
	Virginia	18	Washington	29	
	Arizona	19	Colorado	30	
D	Kansas	19	Montana	31	D
I	Ohio	19	Utah	31	I
S	Oklahoma	19	Iowa	32	S
C	California	20	Indiana	33	C
R	Louisiana	20	Massachusetts	33	R
E	Georgia	22	Rhode Island	33	E
T	Minnesota	22	South Dakota	33	T
I	Pennsylvania	22	Nevada	35	I
O	South Carolina	22	New York	35	O
N	Wisconsin	23	West Virginia	36	N
	Alabama	24	Idaho	37	↓
	Nebraska	24	Vermont	37	
	North Dakota	24	New Mexico	40	

SOURCE: *Adapted from: Zimmerman, J. (1983). State-Local Relations: A Partnership Approach. New York: Praeger Publishers*

culture can best be described as "an enduring set of beliefs, values, and traditions about politics which constitutes a general framework of plans, recipes, rules, and instructions for the conduct of political life, especially who gets what, when, and how" (Kincaid, 1980: 91). Tracing historical settlement and migration patterns, Elazar (1966) has classified the types of political culture as moralistic, individualistic, and traditionalistic. Although each type shares common values of the American culture, each has distinct interpretations of those values and has synthesized and manifested them into different political systems.

There are several major themes underlying Elazar's work. The first relates to contrasting views of the fundamental nature of government in society. One view is that of a commonwealth, while a second is that of a marketplace. In a commonwealth, there tends to be a collective or communal pursuit of a "good society," which, although often a vague abstraction, becomes an end unto itself. With such an orientation, issues of substantive justice would prevail. Conversely, in a marketplace, government is an arena in which individuals and groups bargain out of enlightened self-interest. The notion of a "good society" is seldom an end unto itself. As a result, concerns over procedural justice prevail.

A second theme involves how space and territory are defined. To Elazar, there are two principal views. The first view originated in New England and sees territory as the domain of a particular group. A group is free to pursue its own vision of what society should look like. New England towns of the 18th century were primarily built as religious communities wherein each of the inhabitants shared a common belief about the relationship between man and God (Zuckerman, 1971). When members of that community differed in their beliefs from that of their fellow townspeople, their option was often to move and create another community in which their beliefs became dominant. Indeed, much of the early growth in New England occurred in this fashion. The second view of territory is much more heterogeneous. It presumes that many groups will occupy the same territory. Control and power over that territory is a constant competitive battle between groups for dominance.

The moralistic cultural perspective tends to view the world as a commonwealth and territory as the domain of a particular group. Its primary roots are in the covenanted communities of New England and the Puritan/Calvinist religious movements. It is represented by an activist orientation that may or may not involve governments in the search for the "good society." Individuals are expected to engage in that search, making government everyone's responsibility and duty. Government structures become forums in which the issue is the center of debate.

The individualistic cultural perspective is that of the marketplace and a more heterogeneous view of territory. The primary role of government is to provide the process that keeps the economic sphere in order. Government is a business, often organized through a hierarchical party apparatus, that tends to be the arena for professionals and perceives a

Table 5.9   Type of Political Culture by American State

Moral		Individual		Traditional	
Minnesota	1.00	California	3.55	Delaware	7.00
Washington	1.66	New York	3.62	Maryland	7.00
Colorado	1.80	Kansas	3.66	New Mexico	7.00
Iowa	2.00	Massachusetts	3.66	Texas	7.11
Michigan	2.00	Nebraska	3.66	West Virginia	7.33
North Dakota	2.00	New Jersey	4.00	Kentucky	7.40
Oregon	2.00	Wyoming	4.00	Missouri	7.66
Utah	2.00	Pennsylvania	4.28	Florida	7.80
Wisconsin	2.00	Illinois	4.72	Virginia	7.86
Maine	2.33	Nevada	5.00	Louisiana	8.00
New Hampshire	2.33	Ohio	5.16	Oklahoma	8.25
Vermont	2.33	Arizona	5.66	North Carolina	8.50
Idaho	2.50	Indiana	6.33	Tennessee	8.50
Connecticut	3.00			Alabama	8.57
Montana	3.00			South Carolina	8.75
Rhode Island	3.00			Georgia	8.80
South Dakota	3.00			Arkansas	9.00
				Mississippi	9.00

SOURCE: *Adapted from: Sharkansky, I. (1969). "The Utility of Elazar's Political Culture: A Research Note." Polity. Volume 2: pp. 66–68.*

more limited role for the citizen. Although government exists to maximize the preferences of constituents, it also allows for the accumulation of personal gain on the part of actors.

The traditionalistic cultural perspective manifests ambivalence toward the marketplace and an elitist concept of the commonwealth. Its primary roots, historically, are in the South. The fundamental role of government is the maintenance of the existing social order. As such, it is predicated on a hierarchical-ordered class system where government is the responsibility of the elites and the role of lower classes is to be taken care of.

Operationalizing political culture has proved to be a difficult task (Miller, 1991; Kincaid, 1980; Wirt 1991). However, Sharkansky (1969) placed each of the forty-eight states on a continuum from 1 to 9 on the states' dominant political culture. I have converted this continuum into classifications by assigning scores of 1 to 3.5 as moralistic; scores of 3.5 to 6.5 as individualistic; and scores of 6.5 to 9.0 as traditionalistic. The score for each state is reported in Table 5.9.

As was the case with discretionary authority, political culture plays a significant role in defining state and local government systems in the United States. States with a dominant moralistic or traditionalistic culture tend to assume a greater share of fiscal responsibility whereas states with a dominant individualistic culture are more apt to place a greater fiscal role on the shoulders of local governments.

Generally, states with a moralistic or individualistic political culture tend to have higher combined state and local expenditures, whereas states with a traditionalistic political culture tend to have lower overall state and local government expenditures. However, the pattern is very different between the moralistic and individualistic states. Although the total expenditures are equal, states with a moralistic political culture tend to have less economic capacity than states with an individualistic political culture. This observation suggests that a broad sense of the "public good" may well manifest itself in the form of higher expenditures than economic capacity might well have suggested. Although states with an individualistic culture may place greater fiscal responsibility on local governments, that relationship could be on a relatively short leash. The relative importance of the party apparatus as a feature of the individualistic culture (Elazar, 1966) may lead to a more rigid hierarchical structure where both the state and local governments are components of the larger party system.

Competition between levels of government exists in all cultural environments. That the interplay in individualistic states has led to a greater perceived role for local government may not necessarily mean greater discretionary authority on the part of those local governments. Calling upon local governments to play a greater role in the administration of public programs may not be threatening to state officials in that control and conformance is maintained through a more rigid party apparatus. Conversely, Elazar suggests that the role of party is less important in the moralistic culture. As a result, the intergovernmental hierarchy may be less important. Further, the competition between levels of government might be more substantive. It could be difficult, in a moralistic state, to observe its degree of fiscal federalism and conclude whether it represented the state's dominance of local government, or the local's skillful exploitation of the state.

Geo-spatial Dimension

The third dimension I refer to as geo-spatial. Geography plays an important role in defining the relative roles state and local governments play in their respective state systems. As the physical size of the state increases, there is a tendency for local governments to play a greater fiscal role relative to the state government. The same relationship exists with population—as population increases so does the fiscal role of local governments. However, it is conceivable that this larger fiscal role represents the state's skillful use of local governments as administrative agents of the state. Density has the effect of increasing per capita expenditures at both the state and local levels. The notion that greater density could lead to economies of scale and therefore lower expenses is not borne out by the evidence.

The more heterogeneous a state system is, the greater the fiscal role of local governments tends to be. The converse is also true. The more homogeneous a state is the more likely the state government is to assume greater fiscal responsibility. This observation makes intuitive sense. The degree to which a state reflects a relatively shared vision, it is easier for that state to develop a relatively uniform response to demands. Conversely, the more heterogeneous a state, the more each part of the state needs to be able to reflect local needs and priorities.

Systems with larger numbers of local governments tend to be more fiscally centralized than systems with smaller numbers of local governments. Further, as the average population size of the local governments increases, so does the fiscal role of the state. It is conceivable that this observation represents the skillful fiscal use of the state government financing mechanism by local governments in pursuit of their goals and objectives.

Economic Dimension

Greater or lesser economic capacity of a state system has been advanced as the primary determinant of differences in systems by a number of authors from Fabricant (1952) to Dye (1966) to Peterson (1979; 1981). The underlying assumption is the more healthy the economy, the more active the government. Clearly there is a strong relationship between economic capacity and differences in state systems. Overall, state systems with greater economic capacity spend more. However, within that general observation, the economic capacity does not drown out the other dimensions. Indeed, it takes all four dimensions to explain how the American system works.

The Metropolitan Power Diffusion Index

Although the preceding discussion provides a good analysis of the different systems of local government, the unit of analysis is still the state.

Metropolitan regions are generally contained within a state, but are, nonetheless, different from the state government. What is needed is a measure that directly compares and contrasts the distribution of authority and power within the metropolitan regions. After reviewing and summarizing academic efforts to undertake metropolitan regional comparisons, I will outline my own methodological approach. I call it the "Metropolitan Power Diffusion Index" (MPDI).

Efforts to provide some comparative analysis of governmental power or diffusion in metropolitan areas in the United States fall broadly into one of two methodological approaches. Generally, these methods assert that they are trying to measure fragmentation. Consistent with those efforts, earlier published versions of the MPDI were referred to as a "Metropolitan Fragmentation Index" (Miller, 1999; Weaver, Miller and Deal, 2000). However, fragmentation is too value-laden a term. It presumes that something is broken and ought to be repaired. Such prescription is not my intent. Hence, I have renamed the index to reflect the more neutral concept of diffusion.

The first methodology is a simple process of counting the governments, either in absolute terms or on some per capita basis. Dolan (1990: 28) defines local government fragmentation as the proliferation of government units that may exist within a given region. This work is built on the earlier work of Goodman (1980), who identified four types of fragmentation—two of which were counts of 1) incorporated municipalities and 2) special districts, public authorities, and school districts.

Hill (1974), in an effort to assess inequality among residents of metropolitan areas, used the number of municipalities and the number of municipalities per capita as measures. Bollens (1986) was also interested in inequality in metropolitan areas and used the number of non-center city municipalities over 10,000 population per 100,000 non-center population as a measure. Zeigler and Brunn (1980) used the number of local governments per 100,000 in their effort to distinguish geo-political patterns of the frostbelt regions (northeast and midwest) from the sunbelt regions (south and west). Hawkins (1971) developed a measure of fragmentation as total governments per 100,000 population in an effort to determine the impact of that fragmentation on the cost of government. Parks and Oakerson (1992) use governments per 10,000 as a "fragmentation score."

The idea that the more governments there are, either in absolute or per capita terms, the more power is diffused in the region has merit. Creating a government puts in play another actor with political power and rights of entry into the decision-making process. However, one significant problem is that it fails to provide a measure of the role each government plays in or contributes to the region. As such, having a significant number of governments that exist "on paper" can over-inflate that statistic as a meaningful indicator.

Indeed, several of the works cited above attempted to address this weakness. Dolan tried to compensate by introducing the concept of "fiscal dispersion fragmentation," defined as "the standard deviation of the per capita expenditures of the governments in the region under study." Bollens added the percentage of non-central city population that live in incorporated municipalities with over 10,000 population as a measure. Zeigler and Brunn attempt to reduce several dimensions into a single index by using the number of governments as a direct proportion and the percentage of the population living in the center city as an inverse proportion.

Regardless of the efforts of these authors to add a political dimension, none of the studies added a time dimension. This generally can be understood in that the authors were using their measure of fragmentation to explain some other condition in metropolitan areas of the United States. As such, they fail to assess how power is changing over time.

The second approach applies a methodology from the business sector as it relates to the market share of firms in a competitive arena. It is often referred to as the Hirshmann-Herfindal Index (HHI). This approach has a simple premise—power is market share. If one firm has 90 percent of the market, whether 50 players or 5 players share the remaining 10 percent is of marginal interest. These small players have little "political power." Indeed, Scherer and Ross (1990: 72; see also, Shepherd, 1985) observe, "The HHI weights more heavily the value for large firms than for small." The methodology employed is to use the squared percentage of each player's share of the market. As that applies to local governments in a metropolitan area, some measure of expenditures on some array of public services usually substitutes for sales by the firm.

Lewis (1996) employs a variation of this approach in his political fragmentation index. Using the sum of the squared percentages of total expenditures in relation to the degree of expenditures, this index creates a single number that is more sensitive to the total level of expenditures than to the distribution of those expenditures within the metropolitan area.

Although both methodologies capture important principles—the first a measure of political power and the second a measure of economic power—they need to be combined so that both may make a contribution to the resulting scale. As such, the problem has now been boiled down to a mathematical one. How does one mathematically represent these two perspectives on a single scale? A colleague of mine suggested that the square root of the squared contributions could be substituted for the square of the contributions. Whereas the square of the percentage contributions has the impact of exaggerating the contribution of the larger players, the square root of the percentage contribution has the impact of giving greater mathematical value to the smaller units. Basing the scale on the percent contribution of each player serves to reflect the economic dimension while using the square root of that contribution serves to reflect the political dimension of power derived from the semi-sovereignty of political jurisdictions in a metropolitan environment.

In the process of using the squared-percentage approach (HHI), the resulting scale ranges from 0 to 1. The closer to 1, the greater the concentration of market power. Hence, a low score represents a more diffused system. By switching to the square root, the scale starts at 1 and goes, theoretically, to infinity. Like the first scale, 1 represents pure concentration or one player with 100 percent of the market. Higher numbers, however, represent diffusion.

Without delving too deeply into the mathematics, I have developed an example that is summarized in Table 5.10. Suppose there are two regions (A and B). In Region A there are six governments; in Region B, twelve. Total local government expenditures in both regions are $1,000,000, of which $900,000 (or 90 percent) is spent by the largest government in the each region. In Region A, there are 5 smaller governments that each spend $20,000 while in Region B there are 11 smaller governments that each spend $9,091.

If we compare three common measures of diffusion, we can reach three different conclusions about the distribution of power within those regions. Method 1 is to simply count heads. Region A has 6 and Region B has 12. However, to conclude that Region B is twice as diffuse as Region A would be erroneous. In both regions, one government makes 90 percent of the expenditures.

Method 2 is the Herfindal approach (HHI) that is the square of the percentage contribution of each government. That computation generates an index score of .812 for Region A and .811 for Region B—a virtual tie. However, to conclude that Region B and Region A are equivalent would be erroneous. One region has twice as many governments as the other.

Table 5.10   Theoretical Comparison of the Diffusion of Power Measures in Two Regions

Region A		Region B	
Government 1A	$900,000	Government 1B	$900,000
Government 2A	$20,000	Government 2B	$9,091
Government 3A	$20,000	Government 3B	$9,091
Government 4A	$20,000	Government 4B	$9,091
Government 5A	$20,000	Government 5B	$9,091
Government 6A	$20,000	Government 6B	$9,091
		Government 7B	$9,091
		Government 8B	$9,091
		Government 9B	$9,091
		Government 10B	$9,091
		Government 11B	$9,091
		Government 12B	$9,091
Total	$1,000,000		$1,000,000
Method 1 (Count)	*6*	*1*	*2*
Method 2 (HHI)	*0.812*		*0.811*
Method 3 (MPDI)	*1.656*		*1.997*

SOURCE: *David Miller*

Method 3 is the Metropolitan Power Diffusion Index (MPDI) that is the square root of the percentage contribution of each government. That computation generates an index score of 1.656 for Region A and 1.997 for Region B—a 21 percent difference. Because Region A's score is closer to 1, it can be said to have a greater concentration of power and, because Region B's score is higher, it can be said to be more diffuse than Region A.

The MPDI has been tested against other measures of diffusion. Paytas (2001) assessed its validity compared to other measures of the diffusion of power within a metropolitan region including the absolute and proportional measures mentioned earlier as well as the more sophisticated Lewis model. He concluded that the MPDI was the best measure available for comparative analysis.

Developing diffusion scores for each metropolitan region requires a data source that has information on each governmental jurisdiction within each region. Every five years the Census of Governments develops a summary of expenditures, revenues, and intergovernmental transfers for virtually every local government in the United States. Included in the analysis are all general-purpose governments such as counties, cities, boroughs, towns and townships. Also included are all single purpose governments such as school districts, utility authorities, and special districts. The ability to group the census data into the appropriate Metropolitan Statistical Area (MSA) is possible, at least back to 1972.

Unfortunately, the Census of Governments, although part of the Bureau of Census, has never focused its reporting on MSAs. Hence, categorizing local governments into their respective MSA is not an easy task. Further, the definition and boundaries of a particular metropolitan area may have changed several times since 1972. For our discussion, I selected the boundaries of metropolitan regions as they were defined for 1992. We will look at the regions in 1992 and 1972 as they were defined in 1992. In other words, the representation of the 1972 data is as the MSA was defined in 1992. Of 336 MSAs in 1992, only 311 could actually be used in the analysis. However, those 311 regions contain slightly less than 33,000 individual governments.

Expenditures serve as an excellent surrogate for political power in a metropolitan region and I have selected those to analyze the MPDI. The act of making expenditures is a representation of choice in that it reflects not only the expenditures being made, but also the universe of expenditures that could have been made somewhere else. At a broader level, they also represent a choice of who or what will make those expenditures. To capture the broad range of services traditionally considered to be the domain of local government, the following types of operational expenses were used:

Buildings	Health	Police
Central Staff	Highways	Sewerage
Electric	Hospitals—other	Solid Waste
Finance	Hopitals—own	Water
Fire	Housing	Welfare
Gas	Libraries	
General Government	Parking	

Computationally, the total operational expenditures in any or all of the categories above were added together for each government to generate

Table 5.11 Metropolitan Diffusion Index Scores by Regions-of-States and Population Size, 1972

Size of Region	Region of the United States				Total
	Northeast	Midwest	South	West	
Small	4.59	3.53	2.38	2.74	3.04
Medium Small	4.96	4.30	3.14	3.10	3.69
Medium	6.40	4.48	3.69	3.01	4.23
Medium Large	6.68	6.30	3.36	5.19	4.99
Large	8.12	8.66	4.87	5.00	6.64
Total	5.85	4.25	2.98	3.37	3.83

SOURCE: *U.S. Department of Commerce, Bureau of the Census. Census of Governments, 1972: Government Employment and Finance Files [Computer file]. ICPSR ed. Ann Arbor, MI: Inter-university Consortium for Political and Social Research [producer and distributor], 1975.*

the total spending by those governments. Obviously, some governments, like special purpose districts, might spend in only one of the categories while others, like many city governments, might spend in almost all categories. Each government's percent of the total spending was computed and the square root was taken and added together to generate the diffusion index for each region.

In 1972, the 311 regions of the United States had an average diffusion score of 3.83 (see Table 5.11). The distribution is skewed in that there are a few regions with very high scores. Heading the list is the Philadelphia metropolitan region with a score of 14.3. Rounding out the top seven most diffused metropolitan regions are St. Louis (12.3); Boston (11.2); Pittsburgh (10.7); Scranton/Wilkes-Barre, Pennsylvania (9.3); Minneapolis/St. Paul (8.5); and Chicago (8.3).

At the other end of the scale is the Midland, Texas metropolitan region with a score of 1.3. Rounding out the top seven most concentrated metropolitan regions are Owensboro, Kentucky (1.4); San Angelo, Texas (1.4); Jackson, Tennessee (1.5); Odessa, Texas (1.5); Las Cruces, New Mexico (1.5) and Tucson, Arizona (1.6).

The index is statistically sensitive to population. Small metropolitan regions (those under 250,000 population) have the lowest average diffusion score (3.04). Conversely, the largest metropolitan regions (those over 2,000,000 population) have an average score over twice as large as the small metropolitan regions (6.64).

The region of the United States in which the metropolitan region is located also appears to have an impact on the diffusion score.

Table 5.12   Metropolitan Diffusion Index Scores by Regions-of-States and Population Size, 1992

Size of Region	Region of the United States				Total
	Northeast	Midwest	South	West	
Small	4.99	3.75	2.61	2.99	3.29
Medium Small	5.43	4.67	3.31	3.35	3.97
Medium	7.22	4.77	3.92	3.11	4.55
Medium Large	7.04	6.96	3.56	5.85	5.39
Large	8.93	10.36	5.61	5.71	7.59
Total	6.39	4.62	3.22	3.69	4.16

SOURCE: *U.S. Department of Commerce, Bureau of the Census. 1992 Census of Governments, Finance Statistics (Preliminary) [CD-ROM]. Washington, DC. April 1996*

Metropolitan regions in the northeast are the most diffuse with an average MPDI of 5.85. The midwest metropolitan regions are the next most diffused with an average score of 4.25. Conversely, the metropolitan areas of the south are the least diffused with an average score of 2.98. The west's metropolitan regions tend to look like the south with an average score of 3.37.

At the intersection of metropolitan region population size and region-of-states are several interesting anomalies. Although the northeast generally has higher scores than other regions, large metropolitan regions in the midwest are more diffused than their northeast counterparts. Secondly, although the south has generally more concentrated metropolitan regions, medium and medium-small regions in the west tend to be more concentrated than those in the south. Finally, in all regions except the west, the large metropolitan regions tend to be substantially more diffused than smaller size metropolitan regions within that particular region-of-states.

The above analysis has simply established a base line for us to compare changes over time. By 1992 the mean score for the 311 metropolitan regions had increased from 3.83 to 4.16—an 8.6 percent rise in the index (see Table 5.12). More importantly, 248 metropolitan regions, or 80 percent, had an increase in the score toward greater diffusion of power. An immediate response would be to assume that this diffusion would follow population. As population increases, so should the index. However, the correlation between population change and MPDI score change was found to be statistically insignificant ($r=0.053$).[2] Two other factors seem to contribute more to the change in MPDI than population. The first is an increase in the absolute number of governments and the second is that suburban governments, which have experienced the bulk of the population growth in many of the metropolitan regions, are playing a greater financial role in the delivery of public services.

The Philadelphia metropolitan region continued to have the highest score on the index at 15.4. St. Louis and Boston retained the second and third positions respectively. Chicago jumped from 7th to 4th with a 46.1 percent increase in its score from 8.3 to 12.1. Pittsburgh, Scranton/Wilkes-Barre, Pennsylvania and Minneapolis/St. Paul round out the top seven most diffused metropolitan regions in 1992.

The greatest absolute change in the index occurred in the Chicago metropolitan region—3.82 points. Houston and St. Louis were next with a 2.07 increase in their scores. Those regions were followed by Lake County, Illinois (1.94) and Joliet, Illinois (1.85). Chicago's 46 percent increase in the index made it the most deconcentrating metropolitan region during the 1972 to 1992 period. Five other metropolitan regions also had a greater than 40 percent increase in their score. Those regions were Houston (44 percent); Galveston, Texas (44 percent); Tuscaloosa, Alabama (42 percent); Greeley, Colorado (42 percent); and Midland, Texas (41 percent).

Two significant trends should be noted as the population size of metropolitan areas relates to those changes. Initially, size is not statistically significant. Indeed, all population groups, with one exception, are deconcentrating at approximately the same rate. Small metropolitan regions diffusion score grew by 8.2 percent; medium-small and medium size regions by 7.6 percent; and medium-large metropolitan regions by 8.0 percent. The outliers were large metropolitan regions where the rate of increase was 14.3 percent. This growth rate may suggest that areas that already have a high diffusion score are more apt to deconcentrate power faster than areas that are not as diffused. This observation is supported by the score changes of the 75th percentile metropolitan areas in the medium-large and small metropolitan areas. These regions, relative to their population groups, have comparably higher diffusion scores. They are also experiencing more accelerated growth in their scores—14.5 percent and 10.8 percent respectively.

Region-of-states is also not significantly associated with changes in the diffusion index. Diffusion index scores for the northeast metropolitan regions grew by 9.2 percent. The midwest regions grew by 8.7 percent. Metropolitan regions' diffusion in the south grew by 8.1 percent and the

Table 5.13   Metropolitan Diffusion Index Group Membership by Region of the United States, 1972

	Region of the United States				
	Northeast	Midwest	South	West	Total
Highly Centralized		1	26	10	37
Moderately Centralized	2	21	42	15	80
Slightly Decentralized	8	19	33	17	77
Moderately Decentralized	10	26	17	5	58
Highly Decentralized	15	16	4	9	44
Super Decentralized	11	4			15
Total	46	87	122	56	311

SOURCE: *U.S. Department of Commerce, Bureau of the Census. Census of Governments, 1972: Government Employment and Finance Files [Computer file]. ICPSR ed. Ann Arbor, MI: Interuniversity Consortium for Political and Social Research [producer and distributor], 1975.*

scores for west metropolitan regions by 9.5 percent. Although statistically insignificant, the implications are far from insignificant—metropolitan America is deconcentrating power regardless of geographic location.

In an effort to interpret the changes that are occurring in diffusion of power, I have grouped the metropolitan regions into six groups. MPDI scores falling between 1 and 2 are classified as centralized. Scores between 2 and 3 are classified as slightly centralized. Those that fall between 3 and 4 are classified as slightly decentralized. Scores of 4 to 5 are called moderately decentralized. Scores between 5 and 7.5 are classified as highly decentralized and those above 7.5 as super decentralized.

In 1972, 12 percent of the metropolitan areas were classified as centralized and 4.8 percent were super decentralized (see Table 5.13). Of the centralized regions, 36 of 37 were located in the south or west. Conversely, all 15 of the super decentralized regions were located in the northeast and midwest.

I have made another grouping of the metropolitan regions to capture the diffusion trend between 1972 and 1992. For this analysis, five groups were created depending on the rate of change in a metropolitan region's diffusion score. Those metropolitan regions with a diffusion score that decreased 5 percent or more were classified as centralizing; those with a score that decreased less than 5 percent were classified as slow centralizing.

Conversely, those with an increase in their diffusion score of less than 10 percent were labeled slow decentralizing; those with increases of 10 to

Table 5.14   Metropolitan Diffusion Index Trend Group Membership by Region of the United States, 1972–1992

	Region of the United States				
	Northeast	Midwest	South	West	Total
Centralizing		5	16	7	28
Slow Centralizing	3	18	13	1	35
Slow Decentralizing	24	34	41	16	115
Rapid Decentralizing	15	20	33	22	90
Super Decentralizing	4	10	19	10	43
Total	46	87	122	56	311

SOURCE: *U.S. Department of Commerce, Bureau of the Census. Census of Governments. Finance Statistics (Preliminary) [CD-ROM]. Washington, DC. April 1996 U.S. Dept. of Commerce, Bureau of the Census. Census of governments, 1972: Government Employment and Finance Files [Computer file]. ICPSR ed. Ann Arbor, MI: Inter-university Consortium for Political and Social Research [producer and distributor], 1975.*

20 percent were labeled rapid decentralizing; and those with a greater than 20 percent change were labeled as super decentralizing. The results of that analysis by region are reported in Table 5.14.

As previously mentioned, 80 percent of metropolitan regions fell into a decentralizing category. Conversely, only 63 regions were centralizing. Only 6.5 percent of the northeast and 14.3 percent of the west regions fell into a centralizing category. Over 26 percent of the midwest metropolitan regions were centralizing as were 24 percent of the southern regions. On the other side of the scale, 42.8 percent of the regions in metropolitan America fell into the rapid or super decentralizing categories. The percentage of south and west metropolitan regions that fell into this category exceeded the northeast and midwest. Indeed, 57.1 percent of west regions and 42.6 percent of south regions experienced a growth in their diffusion score of greater than 10 percent. Comparatively, the northeast had 41.3 percent of its regions and the midwest 34.5 percent with an increase in diffusion of greater than 10 percent. So, while the northeast and midwest hold the distinction as the most diffused, the south and the west hold the distinction as the most diffusing.

The highly centralized category had 37 members in 1972 and only 20 in 1992—a significant decline (see Table 5.15). At the other extreme, the number of super decentralized regions increased from 15 to 25—a 67 percent increase in a mere 20 years.

An index score for each service included in the MPDI can also be developed. Those scores for 1972 and 1992 by service area are presented

Table 5.15   Metropolitan Diffusion Index Group Membership by Region of the United States, 1992

	Region of the United States				
	Northeast	Midwest	South	West	Total
Highly Centralized			17	3	20
Moderately Centralized	1	22	42	14	79
Slightly Decentralized	5	13	34	24	76
Moderately Decentralized	10	24	22	5	61
Highly Decentralized	16	19	6	9	50
Super Decentralized	14	9	1	1	25
Total	46	87	122	56	311

SOURCE: *U.S. Department of Commerce, Bureau of the Census. Census of Governments. Finance Statistics (Preliminary) [CD-ROM]. Washington, DC. April 1996*

in Table 5.16. As might be expected, traditional local government services constitute the group of services most highly diffused. In 1972, expenditures on Highways represented the most diffused of services with an average MPDI of 3.61. Other highly diffuse services in 1972 included General Government Expenses, Central Staff, Police, and Finance. At the other end of the index, representing the more centralized services, are Welfare, Hospitals, Gas, Parking, and Electric.

Changes in the index of particular services between 1972 and 1992 present a more detailed explanation of the diffusion of power within metropolitan areas. Most services were more diffused in service delivery in 1992 than in 1972. Highways continued to be the most diffused service at 3.78. However, this represented a relatively modest 4.6 percent increase. The largest absolute change occurred with Fire—a .82 increase representing a 32.9 percent increase. Water, Sewerage, Solid Waste, and Gas increased in diffusion scores between 12.8 percent and 24.7 percent.

The MPDI is an experimental tool that shows promise as a comparative measure across metropolitan regions. I have used it in this chapter to explain how the diffusion of power is changing over time. In Chapter 8 we will use the MPDI in an exploratory fashion to test whether and how this diffusion of power in metropolitan areas makes a difference.

Table 5.16   MPDI Scores for Particular Government Services

Service	Year 1972	Year 1992	Change #	Change %
Highways	3.61	3.78	0.17	4.6%
Central Staff	3.31	3.57	0.25	7.7%
Finance	3.01	3.43	0.42	14.0%
Fire	2.48	3.30	0.82	32.9%
Police	3.18	3.27	0.10	3.0%
General Gov't	3.51	3.25	(0.26)	-7.5%
Water	2.60	3.24	0.64	24.7%
Sewerage	2.54	2.93	0.39	15.3%
Solid Waste	2.45	2.92	0.47	19.3%
Buildings	2.59	2.82	0.23	8.8%
Libraries	2.18	2.29	0.11	5.1%
Housing	1.50	2.12	0.62	41.6%
Health	1.88	2.01	0.13	6.9%
Welfare 4	1.67	1.64	(0.03)	-1.9%
Electric	1.32	1.43	0.10	7.8%
Parking	1.47	1.39	(0.07)	-4.9%
Gas	1.22	1.36	0.14	11.8%
Welfare 2	1.43	1.31	(0.12)	-8.3%
Welfare 1	1.33	1.29	(0.04)	-3.0%
Hospitals - own	1.31	1.24	(0.07)	-5.6%
Welfare 3	1.34	1.16	(0.18)	-13.5%
Hospitals - other	1.23	1.10	(0.14)	-11.0%

SOURCE: *U.S. Department of Commerce, Bureau of the Census. Census of Governments, 1972: Government Employment and Finance Files [Computer file]. ICPSR ed. Ann Arbor, MI: Inter-university Consortium for Political and Social Research [producer and distributor], 1975. U.S. Department of Commerce, /Bureau of the Census. 1992 Census of Governments. Finance Statistics (Preliminary) [CD-ROM]. Washington, DC. April 1996*

Notes

1. Judge Dillon (1911) wrote extensively on the issue of the proper role of local governments in the United States and interested readers are encouraged to read his commentaries.

2. A correlation statistic [r] is a number that ranges from –1 to +1 and represents the correlation or association of any two variables. A score of –1 indicates that the two variables are perfectly correlated in the opposite direction—as one goes up the other goes down. A score of +1 indicates that the two variables are perfectly correlated in that they both go up or down in the exact same relationship to each other. A score of 0 means that there is no relationship between the two variables.

6

The Classic Debate in the
Organization of Metropolitan Regions

In the preceding chapters we have addressed the issue of how a metropolitan region is governmentally organized, and concluded that law allows states to make that determination and that practice has defined it. I would like to turn to a theoretical discussion based on what ought to be the structure of local governance in a metropolitan region.

It would be helpful for this discussion if there were a "theory of local government." However, as MacKenzie (1961: 1) states, "There is no theory of local government. There is no normative general theory from which we can reduce what local government ought to be; there is no positive general theory on which we can derive testable hypotheses." Benjamin (1980: 73–74) asserts, "The absence of theory must be identified as the major problem in the study of local government. Without theory, contradictory conclusions and policy recommendations may be reached, sometimes from the same data." Walker (1986: 86) comments that "perhaps the greatest weakness of local government today is the absence of a theory that describes and interrelates the operational, political, and jurisdictional roles of local governments."

Explanations for this absence of theory are plentiful. Syed (1966) suggests that there exists, on the one hand, a popular image of local governments culturally traceable to Jeffersonian values of a "good" republic built from the bottom up, and a more centrist official image embodied in legal doctrine, on the other. Schambra (1982) sees these two images in a dialectic and historical contradiction extending back to the positions of the Federalists and anti-Federalists in the late 18th century (see also Jillson, 1988). Frug (1980) maintains that the American political system plays one image against the other based on changing values and fears. Mansbridge (1980) considers the former image as face-to-face or unitary democracy and the latter as pluralistic or adversarial democracy and that the inability to know and use the appropriate form of democracy in a particular context creates a constant tension and an inability to resolve that tension.

As a result, we do not have a theory of local government, but two theories. The first, which I refer to as the "metropolitan region as an organic whole," generally reflects the notion of a collectivist-rational approach to organizational design. The second, which I refer to as the "polycentric region," generally reflects an individualistic-rational approach to organizational design. Interestingly, both of these perspectives have had major books published recently. Reflective of the former is a publication of the National Research Council (1999), while the latter is a series of readings edited by McGinnis (1999).

The Metropolitan Region as an Organic Whole

With the ebb and flow of political theory has come the notion of a centralized metropolis. Within the last century, there are three distinct periods in which the notion has had its greatest currency. With the first wave of decentralization from the city in the early 1900s came a corresponding movement within planning circles that recognized inherent problems with that movement away from the central city. The solution, to planners, was self-evident and is embodied in George Hooker's statement, "The enlarging of the city to match the real metropolitan community is the natural method of dealing advantageously with metropolitan city planning problems" (1917: 343).

A second wave of interest in metropolitan regions took place in the 1960s and 1970s. It was rooted in the post World War II scale of urban living that extended far beyond the existing metropolitan periphery, such that the notion of an "urban field" was replacing the traditional concept of city and metropolis (Friedman and Miller, 1965). As suggested by Keating (1995), this interest in the metropolitan area corresponded with the rapidly expanding role of government and the establishment of America's version of the modern welfare state. As a result, this interest bundled together political theories of metropolitan organization and an activist social welfare role of the state into a unified theory. To advocate one was to advocate the other.

The third wave of interest occurred in the middle of the 1990s. It surfaced primarily as a reaction to the globalization of the world economy, to the decay of center cities and the inner ring of suburbs surrounding those cities, and to the growing disparities in economic wealth between jurisdictions in those metropolitan areas (National Research Council, 1999). This "iron law of urban decay" occurs, it is argued, as an artifact of our systems design (fragmentation) and not as the natural order of events (Luria and Rogers, 1999).

Much of the regionalist movement of the latter part of the 20th century is built on the notion that there exists an emerging world economy in which new organizations of different scale are needed. It is built on the assumption that a great paradox is shaping the organization of society on a global basis. This great paradox is captured in Benjamin Barber's statement, "The planet is falling precipitously apart and coming reluctantly together at the very same moment" (Barber, 1995). On one hand, there is a deconcentration of society occurring that can be referred to as the return to tribes. On the other hand, the new economic order is forcing a new globalism as it is creating a planet of metropolitan regions.

Why metropolitan regions? The answer to that question lies in a set of assumptions about the future economy of the planet. Michael Porter (1998: 78) has coined the term "clusters" to describe how businesses will prosper in the future. Unlike prior economic periods where businesses simply move to areas of low production cost, businesses must now seek out areas where there exists a critical mass of businesses in a particular field that enjoy competitive success through the geographic concentration of interconnected companies and institutions. Clusters like Silicon Valley and Hollywood are Porter's classic examples of clusters that exist and are supported by local things that further support the existing cluster, the monopoly which that cluster has in the world order, and the ability of that cluster to expand and support the local economy.

Henton (1997) has identified four features of clusters, or "regional habitats," that make them valuable to businesses. The first is easy access to specialized workforces. Obviously, given high concentrations of jobs in a particular field, it is easier for businesses to obtain the workforce necessary to undertake its functions. Second, clustering enhances the research and commercialization capacity for those businesses in the cluster. Third, clustering creates important innovation networks that allow the local businesses to retain a competitive advantage over the competition. Finally, clustering creates "a unique business infrastructure" that supports the companies in ways that creates a working relationship between the institutions within a region and the agglomeration of businesses in that region.

Several of the essential ingredients of a successful cluster require the political institutions of the region to work together in ways that enhance the competitive position of the cluster. For instance, Porter (1998: 80) identifies the need for a high-quality transportation infrastructure, well-educated employees and a tax and regulatory environment that address-es the specific needs of that cluster[2]. Hence, the need for regionalism in support of that cluster is established.

Economic clusters generally do not follow geo-political boundaries. Further, existing geo-political boundaries are either too large (states) or too small (cities, counties). Indeed, most clusters are bigger than any sin-gle municipality but seldom constitute a whole state. Many clusters over-lap state boundaries like the pharmaceutical cluster of eastern Pennsylvania and northern New Jersey; the hospital management cluster of Nashville and Louisville; and the financial services cluster of the New York City metropolitan area (Porter 1998: 82). Logically, a new geo-political structure is necessary to match the cluster structure of the glob-al economy. That match is the metropolitan region.

The organic whole argument has been supported by research that has attempted to establish an interdependent link between the center city and the surrounding suburbs (Downs, 1994; Lebedur and Barnes, 1992, 1993; Savitch et al 1993, National Research Council, 1999). The essence of the argument is that the success of a metropolitan region is based on the improving economic health of both the center city and the suburbs. The stronger the economic growth of the center city, the stronger the econom-ic growth of the suburbs. Conversely, an economically distressed center city adversely impacts the economic growth of the suburbs. The image that is portrayed is one of a heart pumping oxygen to the body. The cen-ter city serves as the place where people migrate from outside the region. As they become more affluent, they move to the suburbs. Successful sub-urbs are therefore dependent on new immigrants to the metropolitan region as their future residents. Adams et al (1996) demonstrates that the out-migration from economically weaker center cities tends to be into suburban areas in *other* metropolitan regions. Conversely, out-migration from economically stronger central cities tends to be into the suburbs of *that* metropolitan region.

The economic reasoning behind the metropolitan region as an organic whole has a social equity counterpart. Its elucidator is David Rusk (1993, 1999). Rusk predicates his reasoning on the notion that poverty and its resulting social dysfunctions are made worse by its concentration and that the elimination of poverty is a necessary end of any society. Poverty begets poverty. Mix poor children in middle-class neighborhoods and there is a good chance they will grow up middle-class. Put poor children in poor neighborhoods and there is a good chance they will grow up poor. Unfortunately, as Rusk argues, decentralized local government structures and suburban growth patterns foster concentrations of poverty, particularly in center cities. Those governments with the highest concentrations of poor are becoming increasingly unable to cope with the costs of that concentrated poverty. Deconcentrating poverty, according to Rusk, is a regional responsibility that requires regional institutions, particularly in the areas of land use planning, fair-share housing plans, and revenue-sharing programs.

Unfortunately, according to Rusk, an alternative to his regional program to disperse poverty throughout a metropolitan region has been the adopted American strategy of the last 30 years—simply rebuild poverty neighborhoods. The federal government has embraced this strategy by investing billions into rebuilding inner city neighborhoods. It has fostered over 2,000 community development corporations (CDCs) that serve to aid in this rebuilding of inner city America. It has allowed the suburbs to stay isolated and to point to this rebuilding solution as official policy. Such a policy is perceived as preferable to opening suburban doors to the region's poor, particularly those poor who are also racially different. Rusk (1999) argues that a contain-poverty strategy has been ineffective. Deriving statistics from the neighborhoods served by 34 "exemplary" CDCs identified by the National Council for Community Economic Development and the Community Development Research Council, Rusk assessed their performance. Two examples capture the losing battle that poverty containment is fighting. Poverty rates for families increased from 23 percent in 1980 to 26 percent in 1990 in neighborhoods served by "exemplary" CDCs formed in the 1970s and from 19 percent in 1970 to 28 percent in 1990 in neighborhoods served by "exemplary" CDCs formed in the 1960s. Average household income as a percent of metro-wide average household income decreased from 64 percent in 1980 to 58 percent in 1990 in neighborhoods served by CDCs formed in the 1970s and from 61 percent in 1970 to 53 percent in 1990 in neighborhoods served by CDCs formed in the 1960s.

Generally, the preferred organizational design of the metropolitan region that flows from this model of the region is one where the integration of local governments is maximized. This can be accomplished either through reducing the actual numbers of governments or by increasing the mandated coordination of those governments by some higher level of government. The metropolitan region is a "well oiled machine" that has minimized its disparities and maximized its external competitiveness.

The Polycentric Region

It has been in the last several decades that the desirability of having many political jurisdictions in a metropolitan area has been advocated from an economic perspective rather than more traditional political arguments (Tiebout, 1956). In what has turned out to be a seminal article, Tiebout advanced the proposition that the more governments that exist in a metropolitan area, the more choices consumers have in selecting a community in which to reside. By creating a "market" for public goods, consumers can vote with their feet.

The broad theory on which Tiebout's musings lie is often referred to as "public choice." Because this view represents a powerful alternative to the organic whole argument, it is important to assess this theory in more detail. In its simplest form, public choice is "the application of methods of modern economics to the study of political processes" (Frey, 1978). It has been viewed as a bridge between the actions of persons in the marketplace and persons in political processes under the assumption that the same individuals act in both arrangements and use similar rules in their actions (Buchanan, 1972). Although the subject matter is political science, the methodology is economics. As such, the actions of persons are presumed to be egoistic, rational, and utility maximizing (Mueller, 1979).

Derived from this view of individuals as the building blocks of society are revised views of traditional political concepts. For instance, politics is the "procedure to come to social (collective) decisions on the basis of individual preferences" and the state is "an instrument for fulfilling collective wants revealed by individuals" (Frey, 1978). Although public choice was developed within the context of modern economic theory, its resonance with historical American political theory has enhanced its ability to impact principles and practices of American metropolitan design.

American political theory, at least at the time of the American Revolution and the subsequent design of its political systems, was based on a contract theory of the state (Frug, 1999; Wickwar, 1970; Syed, 1966). During the nation-state building process of the last thousand years, political theorists have struggled with conceptualizing how the state came into existence. To such theorists as John Locke (1632–1704) and Thomas

Hobbes (1588–1679), before society, man lived in a state of nature. Although Locke and Hobbes differ fundamentally in the reason why, they both theorized that man needed to leave the state of nature and form a society. In the process of forming this society, man entered into a contract with others to create the society. As such, this new government was a collection of individuals expressly brought together by each other to govern themselves. From the Magna Charta to the Mayflower Compact to the Declaration of Independence and to the first words of the American Constitution that say, "We the people of the United States," this notion of society as a contract between individuals runs through American political theory.

Locke's theorizing on the reasons for state formation were of particular interest at the time of the American Revolution, particularly to the principal author of the Declaration of Independence, Thomas Jefferson. Jefferson is often portrayed as one of the strongest historical advocates for small, autonomous local governments (Syed, 1966). To Locke, the state of nature from which man left to form a society was fundamentally a good place. Locke saw the desire to form society as a way for man to enhance and protect his property. As such, government was limited in its activities to enhancing the ability of individuals to accumulate property and to protect the individual from loss of that property. In this capacity, the state was both a servant and subordinate to the individuals who constituted the state. Hobbes, on the other hand, saw the state of nature as evil. This state drove man to form society for his self-preservation. Thus society was one where the responsibility of the state was to protect man from himself and his neighbors. In this capacity, the state had few limits. America's founding was more Lockean than Hobbesian and, as such, permeates American political culture and has been used in the structuring of the American political system.

Public choice, as an economic theory, and the contract notion of the state, as a political theory, have combined to offer a powerful set of working assumptions bolstered by the analytics of economics.[1] The economic framework is built around the postulate that activities are transactions between individuals or groups of individuals. As such, the physical aspects of society are made up of goods or services while events are the activities that surround the transacting of those goods or services. Some events are preferred and the demand for them will usually exceed their supply. Other events are adverse and their supply will usually exceed their demand. Externalities are spillover effects that are not contained within the transaction. Like events, externalities can either be preferred by or adverse to individuals or groups not involved in the transaction. A morning walk downwind from the odors from an old-fashioned paper mill is an example of an adverse externality, while the same walk downwind from a bakery is usually considered a preferred externality.

Because public choice derives from economic theorizing and in particular market-based economics, the action words that are used reflect the transaction basis of the theorizing. Those words are possession, exchange, and use. They are used to identify two primary forms of events. When possession, exchange, and use are easy to discern in a transaction, it generally means that the goods and services involved are divisible, discrete and those not willing to pay can be excluded. Such an event is defined as a private event. It is the classic definition of a market-based economy where a willing buyer will purchase from a willing seller.

When possession, exchange, and use are more difficult to discern, the transaction surrounding the goods or service is often referred to as a public event. In these transactions, the goods or service are not easily divisible, are not discrete, and cannot easily exclude those who are unwilling to pay for the goods or service. When a local community provides police protection, those residents who would not like to receive the service still derive benefit. In the lexicon of public choice, the provision of public goods and services creates the potential for the problem of the free rider.

Given the two types of events, private and public, it is clear from a theoretical perspective that the preferred event is a private one. As public choice has evolved over the years, there has been a tendency to maximize the frequency of private events and to minimize the occurrence of public events. Issues such as defense and common property are clearly necessary public events. However, in the gray area between obvious private events and obvious public events, the preferred model is private.

This preference for private goods over public goods is not based solely on some parsimonious relationship with market transactions. The model of the individual on which public choice is based has two principal components. First, it assumes the individual is rational in that he or she is able to rank all known alternatives in a consistent manner. Second, it assumes that each individual has preferences that affect the decisions he or she makes. This latter assumption is more specifically referred to as self-interest. Under conditions of uncertainty, an individual will consistently choose strategies that will yield the greatest net benefit as weighed by the individual's own preferences.

As it relates to public goods, the actions which individuals take lead to what public choice refers to as the tragedy of the commons. Individuals will maximize their own net welfare by taking advantage of common property or public goods at minimal cost to themselves. There is no theoretical condition under which individuals would not adopt such a maximizing strategy. Further, most public goods would not be provided or would be sub-optimally provided if the funding were strictly voluntary. As such, coercion or taxation is necessary to adequately fund public goods or common property.

There are two innovations implicit in public choice. The first is the notion of market competition. Western economic theory is predicated on the belief that market forces, created through competitive processes, are the optimal means to efficiency and effectiveness. As that relates to governing metropolitan areas, local governments, although body politics, are more like retail businesses in a mall selling a particular bundle of services at a particular cost. Ideally, as a business, each local government would select and price a bundle of services that sufficient numbers of voter-consumers would be interested in receiving such that those voter-consumers would elect to reside within the boundaries of that local government (Ostrom, Tiebout, and Warren, 1961).

Second is the notion that local government needs to price its product at a level that would make the purchase of its services by that voter-consumer economically justifiable. If there were a number of local governments in an area, the ones with the lower cost per unit of desired services delivered would be more successful than others. Such competition would force those non-effective local governments to either replace their bundle of services or reduce what they charge for their bundle of services (Schneider, 1989).

As it relates to the design of local government systems in a metropolitan region, Ostrom (1972) has generated a series of propositions about how such a region ought to be organized and the implications of those organizational designs. Initially, the geographic area that a local government serves depends upon the particular public good or service under discussion. Some services, like fire and education, ought to be in small units while others, like water and waste disposal, ought to be served through larger units. Indeed, special districts and regional institutions are integral parts of metropolitan design. Secondly, there is a price to pay in decreased local elected official responsibility and citizen participation as the local government gets larger. Third, as local governments get larger, those governments will rely more on hierarchical organizational designs, further reducing citizen involvement.

Generally, the preferred organizational design of the metropolitan region that flows from this model is one where the structure of local government has been designed to maximize the individual's preferences through the enhancing of competition among local governments. This can be accomplished by maintaining a healthy number of local governments with boundaries that are defined in economic and not political terms. The metropolitan region is the sum of the activities that serve to enhance the collective preferences of its citizens.

Summary

In this chapter we have explored the two dominant and competing theories about how metropolitan regions ought to be organized. Both perspectives are derived from deeply held convictions about the nature and purpose of man. In the next chapter we will explore how local governments are coordinating activities.

Notes

1. A bridge between economic and political reasoning within public choice literature is the ethical discourse of John Rawls (1972). Rawls draws from Lockean notions about the nature of the state that establishes society as a contract between individuals. He also uses economic reasoning derived from public choice to establish the fundamental rules that would guide such a formation of the state.

2. As an example, counties and municipalities in the Hampton-Newport News, Virginia region have recently formed the Peninsula Workforce Development Center that, according to their promotional material, "supports effective, multifaceted training services for a globally competitive workforce in the region."

7

Defining Regionalism and Approaches to Regionalism

There is emerging a great paradox in the design and functioning of governance systems in metropolitan regions in the United States. At the same time that those regions are becoming more diffuse (as measured by the MPDI), they are becoming more integrated in resolving problems at the metropolitan level. This chapter deals specifically with identifying and exploring the primary ways in which local governments are engaging in regional activities. However, before undertaking that task, the nature of this great paradox needs to be established.

The primary explanation for the paradox results from our moving from thinking about a paradigm centered on government to one centered on governing or governance. Governing is the act of public decision-making and is no longer the exclusive domain of governments. Indeed, governments at all levels, non-profit organizations, and the private sector now work together in new partnerships and relationships that blur sectoral lines. Private businesses, under contract to governments, deliver a wide variety of government programs. Conversely, governments are often managing more private sector firms than public sector employees. Non-profit organizations, often representing organizations of governments, are partnering with governments, private firms and other non-profits to deliver services. Private foundations in many metropolitan regions, utilizing revenues generated from the private sector, are working to finance public, private, and non-profit organizations in the addressing of important regional public problems. The net result is a paradigm that recognizes the formal and informal organizing of institutional relationships that constitute the governing of the metropolitan area.

Indeed, the notion of a large conceptual difference between the study of governments and the study of governance has led Savitch and Vogel (2000, 162–165) to identify five broad organizational approaches that are currently used in metropolitan regions in the Unites States. The first approach is referred to as consolidationist. As represented in regions like Jacksonville, Florida, Indianapolis, Indiana, and Nashville, Tennessee, this approach favors reducing the number of independent local governments and concentrating authority in a small number of large public institutions.

A second approach is referred to as multitiered. The idea that local governments do local activities and regional governments do regional activities is not new. However, rather than refer to those tiers as higher or lower in a hierarchical sense, these tiers are differentiated on the wideness or narrowness of the services being delivered. Small jurisdictions deal with local services like police and fire while larger jurisdictions deal with regional services like transportation and waste removal. Fundamental to this approach is the creation of new and usually large regional institutions to provide those wide services. The Minneapolis/St. Paul region is cited as an example of this approach to regional organization.

A third approach is referred to as linked functions. Unlike the multitiered approach that generally includes the creation of new units of regional government, existing larger units of government are encouraged to deliver public services through inter-local agreements. As an example, Mecklenburg County and the City of Charlotte, North Carolina have negotiated service arrangements wherein the city provides one set of services and the county provides a complementary set.

A fourth approach is referred as complex networks. This approach embraces the notion of large numbers of independent local governments working in both cooperative and competitive relationships that are designed to maximize citizen control and the delivery of services preferred by those citizens. The fifth approach suggested by Savitch and Vogel is called public choice and is very similar to the complex networks approach, but theoretically rejects the notion of regional public interventions in the delivery of public services.

The five general approaches identified by Savitch and Vogel are consistent with our discussion in the last chapter about the two traditions in metropolitan design. The consolidationist, multitiered and linked functions approaches generally reflect the region as organic whole framework while the complex networks and public choice approaches represent the polycentric region framework.

Many efforts to categorize regional strategies have been attempted. Those efforts usually present a long list of cooperative approaches organized from informal cooperation, the easiest to implement, to governmental consolidation, the most difficult (Sparrow and McKenzie, 1983; Walker, 1987; and Stephens and Wikstrom, 2000). The presumption is that the more difficult the strategy, the more desirable it may be in reforming the governance of a metropolitan region.

Let me depart from that more prescriptive approach and suggest that there are four broad forms of metropolitan regionalism. Although we will cover all of the major approaches to regionalism detailed in those easiest to hardest lists, it will be done in a manner that is more descriptive and value-neutral. The first form is coordinating regionalism and deals with the integrated planning of the region as a whole and the consistency of local municipal strategic plans to the strategic plan of the region. The second form is probably the most prevalent and I refer to it as administrative regionalism. It comes in two primary forms—the functional transfer of services from municipal governments to either special districts or to county governments and the day-to-day negotiations between all types of local governments that lead to a myriad of cooperation agreements at an operational level between those governments.

The third form is fiscal regionalism. This form represents a set of cooperative strategies that recognizes the governmental structure of the existing configuration of local governments but creates metropolitan regional funding mechanisms for a wide variety of public purposes. As such, they are relatively recent innovations in metropolitan cooperation. There are three broad types of fiscal regionalism: cultural asset districts, tax and revenue sharing programs, and peaceful coexistence plans.

The fourth form is structural regionalism. This form deals with changing the boundaries of one or more existing units of local government. There are three types of structural regionalism: annexation, city county consolidation, and mergers/consolidations.

In the process of identifying these forms of regionalism, four notes should be made. First, we will only indirectly address the question of why some metropolitan regions are more apt to engage in certain regional activities than other regions. An interesting method to explore this question has been developed by Foster (1997). Foster argues that there is a series of impulses that affect whether a region responds in a central-ized or a decentralized manner to issues confronting the region. Those impulses are natural resources; the extent of similar economies; the extent of central city dominance; the extent of common growth and development experiences; socioeconomic similarities; incentives for shared service delivery; the extent of support for redistribution of resources; political similarities; state and federal policies; and histori-cal factors.

Second, we will not make qualitative assessments of these forms of regionalism. Some acts of intergovernmental cooperation may not nec-essarily lead to greater overall metropolitan coordination. Hamilton (1998) argues that some strategies may promote "regionalism and cooperation" while others may actually promote "independence and autonomy." However, the forms of cooperation generally discussed here are outside the coming together of a couple of municipalities to share a code-enforcement officer.

Third, we will not deal extensively with the role that state and fed-eral actions, either coercive or incentive-based, play in stimulating the movement toward regional approaches. Broadly, most states and fed-eral agencies prefer to see local governments cooperating at the region-al level. At a more coercive-based level, demands in the form of man-dates for improvements in air and water quality have prompted met-ropolitan regions to work together to satisfy state and federal stan-dards. At a more incentive-based level, federal transportation policy has encouraged local governments to work together to identify the appropriate set of projects that ought to be undertaken in that region (Tregoning, 1998). I will simply acknowledge that these pressures from the state and federal governments exert an enormous influence on local governments to cooperate and, are indeed, instrumental drivers of regionalism.

Finally, there is no consensus on whether these regional forms, when taken as a whole, are leading to better governance of our metropolitan regions. Some have argued that the existing organizational design of relatively voluntary cooperation has built sophisticated transportation networks, managed unacceptable spillover effects, and achieved non-conflicting land use patterns in a truly remarkable fashion (Friesema, 1971). Others see important policy issues left unresolved as emerging metropolitan organizations have failed to address even fundamental issues (Berg and Kantor, 1996).

Coordinating Regionalism

Institutionally, most if not all, metropolitan regions have formal organizations of local governments, special districts, and other public and private institutions. Through federal incentives and requirements dating back at least to the 1960s, organizations of local governments now exist that seek to address metropolitan wide issues. The question is no longer whether such an organization exists, but whether that organization engages in meaningful activity. However, that the debate has moved from whether such organizations should exist to the roles and responsibilities those organizations should play does represent a significant movement towards reform.

There are over 450 regional organizations that are represented by their own organization, the National Association of Regional Councils (NARC). NARC defines its membership to include, "multi-purpose, multi-jurisdictional, public organizations *created by local governments* to bring together participants at multiple levels of government to foster regional cooperation, planning and service delivery. They have a variety of names, ranging from councils of government to planning commissions to development districts" (italics added). The organizing principle that these councils be creatures of the local governments in the region reinforces the existing governance structure of the region and also serves to legitimize the council within the context of that structure.

An important recent development in federal-local relations is the Intermodal Surface Transportation Efficiency Act of 1991 (ISTEA). This legislation consolidates federal transportation policy into a relationship between the federal government and a single agency within each of the larger metropolitan regions in the United States. Specifically, each metropolitan region identifies a Metropolitan Planning Organization (MPO) which serves as the institution that decides how federal funds are allocated within that metropolitan region. The effect of such a decision is to invest an MPO with new powers in the highly important game of identifying where transportation improvements would and could occur. For instance, the Southwestern Pennsylvania Commission (SPC), representing nine counties in the Pittsburgh region, is charged with allocating $2 billion in transportation improvements over the next 10 years.

Because most metropolitan areas already had a regional organization when ISTEA was passed, those organizations became the MPOs. However, the organizations that inherited new responsibilities under

ISTEA were primarily voluntary institutions with few formal voting pro-
tocols. Developing democratic decision-making rules has proved to be
the most difficult challenge facing these organizations (Miller and
DeLoughry, 1996; ACIR, 1995). Most regional organizations had developed initially as meet and discuss groups where each government had an
equal voice at the table. For instance, the voting distribution for the SPC
in 1995 gave the core county 24 percent of the vote, even though it contained 58 percent of the population and 64 percent of the market valuation of the region. When the stakes were relatively low, such a distribution was probably tolerable.

However, when an organization skewed heavily to its rural hinter-
lands becomes invested with allocating billions of dollars of development funds, its decisions can reflect its rural bias and an unwillingness
of the organization, on a voluntary basis, to redistribute power. For
instance, in the case of the SPC, the smallest county has 3 percent of the
population and 12 percent of the voting power on the commission and
its representatives are resistant to relinquishing that share of power.

The most frequently used innovation in decision-making rules is the
development of weighted voting structures that reflect the distribution
of population and market value within a metropolitan area. Typically,
MPOs use weighted voting when requested by some percentage of the
jurisdictions. In a survey of 17 of the largest MPOs, more than half had
developed voting structures that reflected the population distribution
of the region (Miller and DeLoughry, 1996: 6). Interestingly, weighted
voting is used infrequently as the mere presence of provisions allowing
for weighted voting appears to encourage compromise without actually having to employ the technique.

The Southeastern Michigan Council of Governments can vote twice
on the same measure, once on the basis of jurisdiction and then again
on a population-weighted vote. Another technique is proportional representation where the number of representatives from each jurisdiction
is based on the population of that jurisdiction. The Mid-America
Regional Council in Kansas City, Missouri and the Northeastern
Illinois Planning Commission in Chicago are representative of this
technique. A third technique is representation on the basis of equal size
population districts that are drawn irrespective of political jurisdictions. Such an approach exists in very few locations, most notably in
Portland Metro, which serves the Portland, Oregon metropolitan
region.

There have been several efforts to assess the degree to which coordination is occurring at the metropolitan regional level. Hitchings (1998) uses three criteria to classify metropolitan regions into four broad categories. The first criterion is whether an official regional plan exists. If the region has a plan, the second criterion is whether a regional organization has been given responsibility to oversee local government compliance with that plan. If the organization has oversight responsibility, the third criterion is whether that regional organization can require changes in local plans to be consistent with the overall regional plan.

The first category of region is considered "ad hoc." In ad hoc regions, local governments work together on specific land-use issues but do not have a written plan that coordinates physical development at the regional level. Although such a region may have a council of governments, that council is primarily a forum for discussion. Most metropolitan regions in the United States fit into this category.

The second category of metropolitan region is "advisory." These regions look much like ad hoc regions except that they do have a regional plan. However, there is generally inadequate means to implement that plan except the willingness of local governments to adhere to the plan on a voluntary basis. Such an example is the Denver, Colorado metropolitan region.

The third category of region is "supervisory." In supervisory regions, a regional body is delegated the responsibility of administering the regional plan. The actual implementation of the plan is still done at the local level, but the regional body oversees compliance and reports progress. Examples of a supervisory region are the San Diego, California and Seattle, Washington metropolitan regions.

The fourth category of region is "authoritative." These regions have both a plan and a regional body. However, this body has a statutory authority to develop the regional plan and then to require changes or force compliance with that plan on the part of local governments. Examples of this type of region are the twin cities of Minneapolis and St. Paul in Minnesota, and Portland, Oregon.

Few regions fall into the supervisory or authoritative categories. Indeed, they have been called "unique" (Stephens and Wikstrom, 1999: 101). Part of this uniqueness lies in the distancing that occurs between the regional organization and the constituent local governments. Rather than organizations of local governments, the Minnesota and Portland organizations are created externally and separate from their local governments.

In Minnesota, the council is appointed by the governor and, in Portland, the executive is directly elected.

States have been taking more aggressive actions to encourage planning and coordination among governments in metropolitan regions. Until recently, Pennsylvania municipalities could plan together, but in the end, each separate municipality had to accommodate all uses within their territorial boundaries. This meant that for the 130 municipalities in Allegheny County, each had to provide industrial, commercial, and housing areas within their individual communities. Recent state legislation now allows municipalities to jointly plan but utilize the entire area of the participating municipalities for the accommodation of all land uses. As a result, a number of communities can treat themselves as a planning district such that some communities may not have any industrial uses at all, while others take on that role for the broader territory.

Administrative Regionalism

The Rise of the Regional Special District

The growth of special districts represents one of the most significant trends in metropolitan organization over the last half of the 20th century. Over 13,000 special districts were created in the United States between 1967 and 1997. This proliferation of governments is seen as further evidence of the fragmentation of metropolitan government. However, embedded within this explosion of governments is the regionalizing of many urban services. In 1977, approximately 25 percent of all special districts had jurisdictional boundaries that were either coterminous with one or more counties or had a service area that was larger than a single county. By 1997, the percentage of these "regional" special districts had risen to 34 percent of all districts (U.S. Bureau of Census, Census of Governments, 1977 and 1997).

The above figures are conservative estimates of the growth in special districts that serve broad regional purposes. Approximately half of all special districts have a boundary that is not coterminous with a single municipality but have a service area smaller than the size of the county. Many of these special districts are collections of municipalities within a metropolitan area that have banded together to deliver a particular public service.

The relative ease of special district formation as administrative regionalism makes intuitive sense at several levels. Initially, special districts are usually created through a long negotiation process among the existing local government actors. Their legitimacy is strengthened through this negotiation process. They are practical solutions to area-wide problems or to mandates imposed by federal, state, or judicial actions as viewed by the local players. As they are created, they are embedded with the traditions, norms, and values of the local institutions that bought them into existence. Secondly, many special districts are creatures or extensions of the existing local governments. Rather than an externally imposed solution that threatens existing geo-political boundaries, these special districts are a mere convenience that reinforces those existing boundaries while allowing for a more efficient and effective delivery of a particular service within the constraints imposed by the existing governance structure.

The Emerging Urban County

Generally, the term "urban county" is used to capture not so much the geographic location of the county, but that the county government plays a significant role in addressing urban issues within the metropolitan area. As discussed earlier, county governments are often viewed as passive. When those county governments take on new responsibilities, particularly those that cut across a number of municipalities, they begin to resemble more active municipal governments. In the process of such a transition, those urban counties serve to further the regionalizing of metropolitan America. Although the growth of the urban county as a form of regionalism is not evident in all parts of the country, its emergence, where it is occurring, has had a significant impact.

The history of the International City/County Management Association (ICMA) captures the emergence of the urban county. This organization represents both professional managers and a value-laden commitment to a set of principles based on the notion that good government is obtainable through the rational application of business principles to public policy problems. Until 1991, the organization was simply known as the International City Management Association. In that year, ICMA changed its name in recognition of the emerging role that the urban county was playing in metropolitan America. Indeed, 16 percent of growth in recognized governments that met ICMA criteria for membership between 1967 and 1995 were county governments even though county governments make up only 8 percent of the total number of municipal and county governments eligible for that membership. In 1984, there were 81 county governments recognized as full council-manager communities and 148 county governments that met the criteria for general management (ICMA, 1984). By 1996, the numbers had grown to 144 and 204 respectively.

Even in states like Pennsylvania that have extensive municipal government systems, county growth can be documented. In western

Pennsylvania, there are 29 county governments and 1,181 municipal governments. In 1970, the 29 county governments spent (in constant 1993 dollars) $869 million while the 1,181 municipalities spent $1,212 million (Miller, 1999). Of combined local government spending, county governments accounted for 42 percent of total spending. Conversely, municipalities accounted for 58 percent of combined local governments spending. By 1993, there was a dramatic shift in the distribution of local government spending. County governments accounted for 53 percent of total spending while municipalities accounted for the remaining 47 percent.

A study by Schneider and Park (1989) of 162 counties located in the 50 largest metropolitan regions found similar results. Comparing 1982 to 1972 expenditures, they found that per capita total expenditures of county governments grew 147 percent from $109 to $265; while per capita city expenditures grew 117 percent from $147 to $319.

Inter-local Agreements

The third type of administrative regionalism is also the most prevalent. It is represented in a myriad of cooperative service arrangements between two or more local governments. It is built on the notion of governments as autonomous units in a metropolitan area negotiating agreements that are perceived to be in the economic interests of the players. Although we see evidence of this form of regionalism on a daily basis, it is usually between have governments, seldom between have and have-not governments. As a result, these cooperative relationships seldom serve a redistributive function.

States are much more likely to create incentive systems that encourage administrative regionalism as opposed to mandating that cooperation. New Jersey's Regional Efficiency Development Incentive Program (REDI) and Regional Efficiency Aid Program (REAP) are representative of this approach. REDI offers grants and loans to help local governments study, develop, and implement new, shared service programs. The State, through the REDI program, budgets $10 million annually to help counties, municipalities, school districts, fire and special districts, and joint meetings identify, prepare, and put into place new inter-local ventures.

REAP reduces the property taxes of residential taxpayers in municipalities, schools, and counties that enter into new shared services agreements. In 2000, taxpayers in 130 municipalities received over $16,000,000 due to the efforts of the municipal, school, and county officials. The program applies to shared service programs that started after July 1, 1997. Interestingly, the financial reimbursement for the shared service program involvement goes directly to taxpayers in the form of tax credits as opposed to intergovernmental transfers to the local government. By so doing, the shared service participation of the local government is more visible to the taxpayer, as is the state's role in encouraging cooperation of local governments.

Fiscal Regionalism

Fiscal regionalism approaches are perceived as attractive because they address metropolitan policy issues in primarily non-threatening ways. Initially, they create the fiscal equivalent of a regional government without the regional government. Second, these mechanisms create the capacity or the authority to distribute benefits from economic growth or to develop growth policies that reflect the distribution of benefits across the metropolitan region.

Third, they represent ways to minimize the worst effects of fiscal mercantilism. Local government reliance on property tax revenues requires those governments to engage in competitive fiscal mercantilism—encouraging only the location of net revenue-producing developments within their boundaries. Such practices exacerbate the difficulties associated with the location of un- or marginally-desirable land uses within a metropolitan region.

Fourth, costs for economic development are not always borne by the government within whose boundary the growth has occurred. Although every government would like to derive economic benefit without cost, the opportunity itself is dysfunctional because a government is rewarded for free-riding. Fiscal regionalism approaches allow for a more equitable distribution of both costs and benefits. Fifth, few means exist whereby governments in a metropolitan region can share in the region's growth, as the only determinant of benefits is location within a particular jurisdiction. Fiscal regionalism approaches create means by which such sharing can occur. Sixth, as will be discussed later, annexation laws create a win-lose outcome for governments—the government getting the new territory wins, but at a significant cost to the government losing the territory. Fiscal regionalism allows for the development of win-win outcomes.

Finally, wealthier jurisdictions are able to provide services with lower tax rates than less affluent jurisdictions. This disparity results in a vicious circle of greater disparity as wealth gravitates to wealth, and the poorer jurisdictions become even less competitive. Over time, the gap between rich and poor communities in a region grows wider. Fiscal regionalism aids in "leveling the playing field."

Cultural Asset Districts

One form of fiscal regionalism is the cultural asset district. This institutional arrangement has emerged in the last several years as a direct result of the deconcentration of population. Even after World War II, the majority of Americans lived and worked in the center city of our metropolitan areas. Cultural and civic activities were usually, and appropriately, financed by the center city. For instance, in 1948, 73 percent of business activity in Allegheny County, Pennsylvania took place within the City of Pittsburgh. For the City of Pittsburgh to be financing the zoo, as an example, was consistent with its economic base and its fiscal capacity. However, by the late 1980s, only 38 percent of business activity conducted within Allegheny County occurred within the City of Pittsburgh. As people and business dispersed to the suburbs, however, they continued to utilize the civic facilities financed by the center city. But the city no longer had the fiscal base to support those services, and non-city residents were becoming the primary users of those facilities. Cultural asset districts, as a form of fiscal regionalism, represent a way for a metropolitan region to finance civic institutions used by the regional public.

Denver and Kansas City are representative of metropolitan regions that have adopted cultural asset districts. In 1988, the Denver region approved the "Scientific and Cultural Facilities District." It is an example of the first wave of this regional approach to public services. Approved with a 75 percent positive vote at a referendum, the district is financed by a one-tenth of one percent increase in the sales tax. The district supports institutions like the zoo, museums, performing arts, and a wide variety of local and regional arts organizations (Hansberry, 1998).

The Kansas City region enacted (again by referendum) a "Bi-State Cultural District" in 1997 to finance the capital and operating costs associated with historic Union Station (Hollis, 1998). Unlike Denver, this district goes out of business in six years. In this respect, it represents the next generation of districts in that it is organized for a specific purpose and, when that purpose is served, the district ends.

Tax-Base Sharing

The second form of fiscal regionalism is tax- or revenue-base sharing. Tax-base sharing is a simple idea: take a regional resource of revenue, such as the property tax or sales tax, and distribute the proceeds to constituent local governments on objective criteria that reflect the needs of

Chart 7.1   The Minnesota Tax-Base Sharing Model

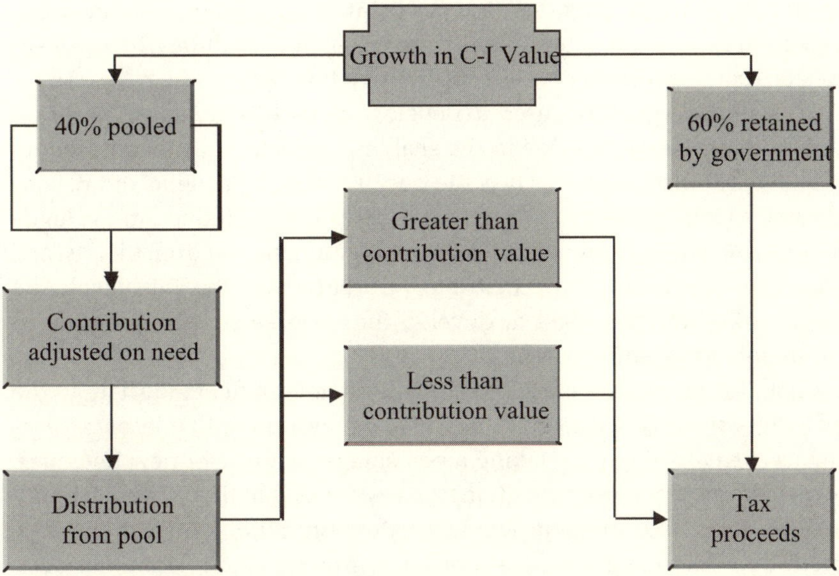

SOURCE: *David Miller*

the region. Its asserted benefits are its more effective and equitable impact on economic development and growth. To the degree that the fragmentation of government services and decision-making in an urban area prevent any rational approach to the distribution of the gains and benefits from development and growth policies, tax-base sharing helps to mitigate the adverse effects of that fragmentation.

The largest and perhaps best known tax-base sharing plan is in the twin cities of Minnesota. The Minnesota model of tax-base sharing has been in place for about 25 years. Today, the program covers 2.5 million people, seven counties, and 200 local jurisdictions, and involves $400 million in tax proceeds. The Metropolitan Council administers the program.

In its simplest form, 40 percent of a municipality's growth in commercial and industrial real estate valuation (shown as "C-I Value" on Chart 7.1) is diverted from the municipality's direct control to a "pool" shared by all municipalities in the region. A uniform millage is applied to this "pooled" value, and the proceeds are distributed back to the municipalities on a need-based formula. Chart 7.1 outlines the Minnesota tax-base sharing model. The amount a government contributes to the pool has no relation to what it will receive in distributions—a participating government may receive much less than it contributes to the pool, and conversely, it may receive substantially more than it contributes. In this fashion, tax-base sharing serves a redistributive function.

Most of the arguments used to develop the fiscal regionalism program in Minnesota were included in the enabling legislation. Although reduction in fiscal disparities has become one of the major benefits of tax-base sharing as implemented in Minnesota, it was not mentioned in the legislation. The explanation for this omission centers on the difficulty associated with the "selling" of redistributive programs at the local level. The arguments that were used to develop the tax-base sharing program in Minnesota are identified below.

First, the plan was a means to allow local governments to share in the growth of the area without taking away any resources that local governments currently enjoy. By taking a percentage of future or new revenues, local governments were not giving up resources that they were currently receiving. Second, the plan would create more rational urban development by minimizing the fiscal impact of private sector locational decisions. Third, the plan would create an incentive system that would encourage all parts of the region to work for the growth of the whole. Fourth, and perhaps most important, the plan would develop regional strategies that employed the existing structure of local governments and local decision-making. Fifth, the plan would assist those communities either in the early stages of development or those facing disinvestments by allocating additional resources to them. In summary, the proponents of this form of fiscal regionalism were supporting the existing structure of local government in the area while recognizing a need to minimize some of the dysfunctions associated with that structure.

Since its inception, the plan has reduced fiscal disparities between jurisdictions. For the period 1987 to 1995, measured inequality in total tax base per capita between jurisdictions was reduced by 20 percent (Luce, 1998: 11). These results were similar to an earlier report that identified a 21.1 percent reduction in fiscal disparities between jurisdictions (Minnesota House, 1987).

Luce's (1998) analysis, although concluding that the program significantly reduces property tax-base inequality, suggests that it may not be as successful in reducing competition for economic development as advocates had promised. Using the frequency of tax increment financing[1] (TIFs) as a measure of heated competition between municipalities, Luce

(1998: 9) noted that 46 of 61 municipalities used 343 separate tax increment financing arrangements (TIFs) in 1991 to underwrite commercial-industrial expansion in their respective municipalities.

Part of the explanation for the more limited impact on competition between jurisdictions is the relatively low percentage (40 percent) of commercial-industrial growth that is pooled. That 60 percent of commercial-industrial growth is retained by the municipality is still a significantly large enough "plum" for a municipality to be willing to compete with a neighbor. Notwithstanding the above caveat, Luce is not suggesting that the existing formula does not reduce competition. Rather, the impact on minimizing competition, although beneficial, is not as apparent as the more obvious fiscal property tax disparity reduction.

The Minnesota experience has also demonstrated that the formula as a redistributive tool works adequately, but is not perfect. The correlation[2] between jurisdictional fiscal need and net distributions from the pool was found to be .58 and the correlation between revenue-raising capacities and net distributions was .78 (Luce, 1998: 14). Part of the explanation for the less than perfect match between fiscal need and actual distributions from the pool is the criterion used to assess fiscal need. A jurisdiction's need is determined by the ratio of its per capita assessed market valuation to the average per capita market valuation of all the other jurisdictions in the pool. The size of the gap between the jurisdiction's average assessed value and that of the pool affects the proportion of proceeds received. A community with 50 percent of the average assessed value of the pool would receive twice its population weight. Conversely, a community with 200 percent of the average assessed value of the pool would receive only half of its population weight. Per capita market valuation is only one of a number of measures that can determine fiscal stress or fiscal need. For instance, large cities may have comparatively high per capita market valuations but need far greater resources to address legitimate community needs. Minneapolis and St. Paul, using a more sophisticated formula for determining fiscal need, were identified as having relatively high need-capacity gaps. However, in 1989, Minneapolis contributed more in pooled value than it received in net tax benefits and St. Paul received only 23 percent of its estimated gap (Luce, 1998: 14).

Efforts to develop a better measure of fiscal need are hampered by the implications that such a discussion would open the door for arguments on whether to have the redistributive components in the formula at all. As could be expected, the notion that a jurisdiction provides more in tax value to the pool than it receives in tax benefits from that pool is not necessarily universally accepted in those communities. Rather than run the risk of diminishing the redistributive impact of the program, it is arguably better to stay with the existing, less-than-perfect measure of fiscal need.

Several efforts have been undertaken to assess the replicability of the Minnesota plan to other states. In 1992, an effort was made to assess the application of the Minnesota tax-base sharing model to the state of Pennsylvania (McQuaid et al., 1992). The state as a whole was selected because uniformity provisions in the state's constitution precluded its application at a sub-state level. Methodologically, the study presumed that the state had adopted a tax-base sharing plan, virtually identical to Minnesota's in 1975, and assessed its impact in 1990. What emerged from that analysis supports the notion that the program does serve a redistributive purpose. Hypothetically, in 1990 dollars, communities in the lowest quartile of fiscal capacity received $7.02 per capita in net proceeds from the pool while those communities in the most affluent quartile contributed, on average, $2.27. Such a distribution led to the conclusion that "the impact would be at a level that would be beneficial to those communities that would be net recipients from the pool, but not catastrophic to those communities that would be net contributors to the pool" (McQuaid et al., 1992: i).

This study also found that the overall effect of the program would be to increase slightly taxes on businesses. However, this effect would be more pronounced in the more affluent communities, making the business tax package more attractive in those communities in greater need (McQuaid et al., 1992: 36).

Finally, the study concluded that population size had little effect on a community's contribution to or distribution from the pool. Smaller, less affluent communities received the same general benefits as their larger counterparts while small, more affluent communities were not as adversely affected as their larger counterparts. Business taxes in smaller communities, regardless of need, were adversely affected by the program (McQuaid et al., 1992: 36). An argument could be made that such an impact has a long-term effect on a metropolitan region in channeling business growth to larger areas already equipped with the infrastructure to support that growth. The trade-off for the smaller jurisdictions is the net benefit in tax proceeds from the pool.

In an effort to assess the impact of tax-base sharing on other metropolitan regions, Luce (1997) simulated the program in the metropolitan areas of Chicago, Philadelphia, Portland and Seattle. Although, in a variety of ways, each region has unique political characteristics, they shared a beneficial impact of tax-base sharing on enhancing the efficiency and equity of the existing property tax system. Interestingly, the Portland region, which had the least inequality in tax base across the region before tax-base sharing was introduced, showed the least beneficial impact of any of the regions analyzed. These findings suggest that the more diffused a metropolitan region, the greater net-benefit tax-base sharing would have on that region.

As in the McQuaid, Bok, Miller and James study, Luce's results confirmed that the richer communities tended to lose a little while the poorer communities gained significantly. On reflection, such an observation makes intuitive sense. If the average before tax-base sharing yield from the richer communities was $100 and that of poorer communities $50, a 10 percent reduction for those richer communities would result in a 20 percent increase for the poorer communities. Indeed, from a political perspective, Luce (1997) found that the total population of the net "winners" (governments whose distributions from the pool exceeded contributions) outnumbered the total population of the net "losers" (governments whose contributions to the pool exceeded distributions) in three of the five regions analyzed.

Actual application of tax-base sharing in other jurisdictions is limited. Based on the Minnesota Plan, jurisdictions in Montgomery County, Ohio, have agreed to pool a portion of future growth in exchange for revenues from an economic development fund (Hollis, 1998). Unlike Minnesota, where some jurisdictions lose more than they contribute, the Ohio plan guarantees, through an economic development fund, that every jurisdiction will be a net beneficiary. If contributions to the tax-base sharing pool exceed distributions from the pool, the jurisdiction will receive more from the economic development fund to compensate.

The Meadowlands Area in New Jersey represents a planned commercial and economic development area that spans 14 separate jurisdictions. In 1972, the State of New Jersey established a commission to develop a master plan for the site. Recognizing that not all jurisdictions would benefit equally from the development, particularly if open and public spaces were to be incorporated, a property tax sharing program was developed for the affected jurisdictions.

A program that captures both forms of fiscal regionalism has been developed and adopted in Allegheny County, Pennsylvania. Mirroring Denver, an asset district has been created to help finance many of the region's cultural and civic institutions; mirroring Minnesota, a redistributive tax-base sharing plan has been adopted that assists in reducing fiscal disparity between rich and poor local governments.

There were a number of issues confronting Allegheny County and the City of Pittsburgh in the early 1990s. Initially, there was a need to correct inequities caused by the City of Pittsburgh bearing a significant financial burden for regional assets. For instance, less than 15 percent of attendees at Pittsburgh Pirate games were city residents, even though the City was the sole public underwriter of the stadium. A second problem was the growing fiscal disparity between the county's richer and poorer communities (Miller et al., 1995). Research had demonstrated that the gap was accelerating. Third, many public and private sector leaders believed that, to be economically competitive, the region needed to address the issue of over-reliance on certain taxes such as those on amusement events, real property, and personal property. Fourth, given the deteriorating fiscal condition of the city, there was a need to stabilize and perhaps increase funding for maintenance of existing assets before those assets depreciated to the point of becoming liabilities to the region. In addition, the region had no real mechanism for the funding or development of new assets. Lastly, given the highly diffused governance structure of the region, it was necessary to establish precedent for future cooperative approaches to the resolution of public problems.

The Allegheny County Regional Asset District was created and funded through an additional 0.5 percent on the sales tax. This funding stream generates more than $60 million annually to provide funding to the region's shared assets. Facilities like the zoo, aviary, libraries, parks, and stadiums are now the fiscal responsibility of the region. The operation of the plan is depicted in Chart 7.2.

Two important regional funding issues have been addressed through this program. First, approximately $40 million is provided to the metropolitan region's assets directly from the sales tax proceeds, replacing funding that had previously been provided to the assets by individual local governments. This transfer of funding responsibility, primarily away from the City of Pittsburgh (the estimated impact is $18 million) and Allegheny County (the estimated impact is $18 million), help to make those governments more fiscally sound and competitive than they would be otherwise.

Second, the asset district provides a more stable and elastic funding base for the region's assets. Initially, approximately $13 million was available annually to increase funding to new or existing assets. This discre-

Chart 7.2   The Allegheny County Revenue Sharing Model

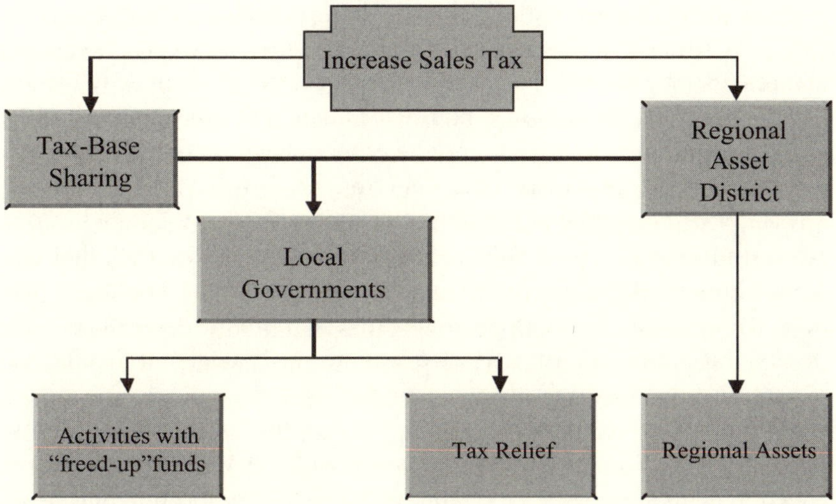

```
                        ┌──────────────────────┐
          ┌─────────────┤  Increase Sales Tax   ├─────────────┐
          │             └──────────────────────┘             │
          ▼                                                    ▼
  ┌───────────────┐                              ┌───────────────────┐
  │   Tax-Base    │                              │     Regional      │
  │    Sharing    ├──────────────────────────────┤      Asset        │
  │               │         │                    │     District      │
  └───────────────┘         ▼                    └───────────────────┘
                   ┌───────────────────┐                    │
                   │      Local        │                    │
                   │   Governments     │                    │
                   └───────────────────┘                    │
                   ┌────────┴────────┐                      │
                   ▼                 ▼                       ▼
        ┌───────────────┐  ┌───────────────┐  ┌───────────────────┐
        │ Activities with│  │               │  │                   │
        │ "freed-up"funds│  │   Tax Relief  │  │  Regional Assets  │
        └───────────────┘  └───────────────┘  └───────────────────┘
```

SOURCE: *David Miller*

tionary portion of the program has grown to more than $20 million in several years.

The "other half" of the legislation that created the first form of fiscal regionalism also brought into existence the second form (Jensen and Turner, 2000). This less publicly visible reform has created a tax-base sharing program second in size only to the Minnesota plan. Through an additional 0.5 percent of the sales tax, more than $60 million is available annually to assist Allegheny County governments in shifting a portion of their funding requirements away from the property tax and other taxes. The distribution is as follows: 50 percent goes to the Allegheny County government, and 50 percent is shared among the participating municipalities in the county. Although all municipalities in the county have a right to participate, the formula used for this distribution targets the less affluent. Per capita distribution under this program ranges from $9.81 in the county's wealthier communities to $18.86 in the most fiscally distressed of the county's communities (Miller, 1999).

Peaceful Coexistence Strategies

The third form of fiscal regionalism involves peaceful coexistence strategies. Particularly in states where territory is divided between incorporated areas, usually run by cities, and unincorporated areas, usually run by counties or townships, fiscal equity arrangements have emerged to address the problems surrounding the economic loss of one governmental jurisdiction when territory transfers from one government to another.

The city of Louisville and Jefferson County, Kentucky entered into a twelve-year agreement in 1986, subsequently renewed in 1998, that has become known as the Louisville Compact. As a center city, Louisville was faced with severe fiscal problems and repeated attempts to consolidate the city and county had been rejected by voters. Although a difficult legal process, the city was poised to engage in a significant annexation campaign that would have serious financial implications for the county. Rather than conduct an adversarial battle with each other, both parties agreed to negotiate a plan for the delivery of services and the funding of those services. Predicated on the assumption that there would be a moratorium on annexation, the parties divided service delivery between them. Services like air pollution control, public health, and planning were assigned to the county. Services like the zoo, museums, and emergency services were assigned to the city. The glue that held the compact together was an agreement to share in tax revenues. The resulting agreement has been beneficial to both the city and the county and, as Savitch and Vogel have suggested, has led to an institutionalizing of cooperation. We will return to Louisville later in this chapter to discuss the latest development in cooperation—the merger of the city and county.

Laws in Virginia represent another example of governments working together to avoid adversarial battles over territory (Hollis, 1998). Agreements entered into by the City of Franklin with Southampton and Isle of Wright Counties are representative. In areas of the counties that are experiencing significant commercial and industrial growth, the city has agreed to no annexation in perpetuity, but has agreed to deliver essential utility services in exchange for a percentage of all local tax revenues collected in the designated areas.

In Michigan, several peaceful coexistence strategies have been developed that create "win-win" outcomes for the state's cities and townships (Beach, 2000). One in particular is Michigan's Land Transfer Act. Rather than annexation, the township conditionally transfers the land that would have otherwise been the subject of annexation to the city in exchange for a share of the tax revenues and state aid. Typically, the agreements are for a 50-year period at which point the land is scheduled to revert back to the township.

Structural Regionalism

Structural regionalism involves boundary change. It takes the existing structure of local government in a region and significantly alters the rules of the game. Whereas the first three forms of regionalism generally retain the existing structure, this form attacks those boundaries such that these reforms "touch the nerve endings of the public" (Thomas and Marando, 1971: 51). Indeed, researchers like Hamilton (1998) have developed two-dimensional scales that capture in one dimension the dichotomy between regional solutions that impact the existing political structure and those that build on that structure.

Annexation

Annexation refers to the process by which territory of one local government is switched to another local government. Although annexation may occur from one incorporated municipality to another, its most general application now is between an unincorporated area and an incorporated municipality. To be unincorporated means that, although there is no formal local government, government services are provided through the county government. As a result, county governments have become the de facto local government for that territory. When the density of that territory becomes such that more sophisticated urban services are required, in states where liberal annexation laws exist, a large (usually center) city seeks to annex that territory. For instance, between 1950 and 1990, Houston, Texas grew from 160 square miles to 540 square miles (Rusk, 1993: 17). The asserted benefit of such annexation is that the center city captures its fair share of the growth that occurs in a region. Houston, through its aggressive annexation policy, captured 43 percent of all growth that occurred between 1950 and 1990, while Albuquerque captured 86 percent of the growth that occurred in its metropolitan area during the same period (Rusk, 1993: 21).

Annexation has occurred in two great waves. The 19th century and the early part of the 20th century saw the first wave of annexation in metropolitan America. Many of the great cities of America were built during this period through annexation and consolidation. Teaford (1979) has referred to those cities as "Imperial Cities." New York City, Chicago, Philadelphia, Boston, Pittsburgh, Detroit, St. Louis, and Cleveland, among others, are products of rapid geographic expansion through annexation and strategic mergers. Although these cities "acquired" additional land over time, there was usually a single point in time when the city grew in one great leap. In 1898, New York City went from 62.5 square miles to 314.7; in 1889, Chicago went from 43.8 square miles to 169.7; in 1854, Philadelphia went from 2 square miles to 128 (National Municipal League, 1974: 65–86).

That imperialism came at a long-term expense. Suburban communities, in many states that were directly experiencing the imperialism of the center city, moved to protect themselves from this expansion through legislation that made annexation difficult, if not impossible. For most of the major cities that grew in the 19th and early 20th century through annexation, their territory today is roughly the same as it was in 1926.

A number of states, particularly in the south and west, have historically had more favorable annexation laws. When the population of the United States after World War II started to move south and west, a second wave of annexation occurred. In those states, annexation has demonstrated an ability to be a powerful form of regionalism and perhaps the most significant and visible form of structural regionalism. During the latter half of the 20th century, its role in the south and west created the closest thing America has to what Neil Peirce (1993) has referred to as "citi-states."

In addition to Houston's territorial growth between 1950 and 1990, other significant changes include Columbus, Ohio, which went from 39 to 191 square miles; Nashville, Tennessee, which went from 22 to 473 square miles; Indianapolis, Indiana, which went from 55 to 362 square miles; Oklahoma City, which went from 50 to 630 square miles; and Atlanta, which went from 32 to 132 square miles (Rusk, 1993).

The second wave may be unofficially over. I selected from each of the 48 contiguous states 77 major cities and assessed their total land area for each decade from 1940 to 1990. In 1940, those 77 cities had a total land area of 3702.1 square miles. Between 1940 and 1950 that total land area grew by 469 square miles for a 12.7 percent increase. The decade of the 1950s saw expansion, through annexation, accelerate to 1552.9 square miles, a 37.2 percent increase. Expansion reached its zenith in the 1960s when 3205.6 square miles were added to the territories of the major metropolitan cities of the United States. This represented a 56 percent increase over that ten year period. The decade of the 1970s saw a marked

Table 7.1 Annexations from 1940 to 1990 in Selected American Cities

| City | No of Cities | 1940 | *Land Areas in Square Miles* | | | | |
			1950	1960	1970	1980	1990
Northeast	14	756.8	776.6	767.0	765.4	779.8	786.8
Decade Change in Square Miles			19.8	(9.6)	(1.6)	14.4	7.0
Percent Decade Change			2.6%	(1.2%)	(0.2%)	1.9%	0.9%
Midwest	22	1,133.6	1,177.2	1,382.0	2,084.3	2,498.1	2,568.4
Decade Change in Square Miles			43.6	204.8	702.3	413.8	70.3
Percent Decade Change			3.8%	17.4%	50.8%	19.9%	2.8%
South	27	940.3	1,277.4	2,272.0	4,423.3	5,059.0	5,236.2
Decade Change in Square Miles			337.1	994.6	2,151.3	635.7	177.2
Percent Decade Change			35.9%	77.9%	94.7%	14.4%	3.5%
West	14	871.4	939.9	1,303.0	1,656.6	1,887.8	2,277.7
Decade Change in Square Miles			68.5	363.1	353.6	231.2	389.9
Percent Decade Change			7.9%	38.6%	27.1%	14.0%	20.7%
United States	77	3,702.1	4,171.1	5,724.0	8,929.6	10,224.7	10,869.1
Decade Change in Square Miles			469.0	1,552.9	3,205.6	1,295.1	644.4
Percent Decade Change			12.7%	37.2%	56.0%	14.5%	6.3%

SOURCE: *David Miller*

decline in the rate of expansion. Although an additional 1295.1 square miles were annexed, those annexations represented a much more modest 14.5 percent increase. The rate of expansion further declined in the 1980s when only 644.4 square miles were annexed, representing a 6.3 percent increase.

Regional variation in annexation is highlighted in Table 7.1. The 14 cities in the northeast were virtually the same size in 1990 (786.8 square miles) as they were in 1940 (756.8 square miles). A large number of these cities were the imperial cities of the 19th century that were precluded by law from further expansion. The midwest followed the pattern of the United States in general with the peak expansion period during the 1960s (702.3 square miles). By the 1980s, the midwest cities grew by only 2.8 percent. The south had cities that experienced the greatest increase in physical size. The cities in the sample had a land area of 940.3 square miles in 1940 and 5,236.2 square miles in 1990. Indeed, approximately 60 percent of the total land area increase in the sample cities occurred in the 27 cities of the south. That expansion occurred primarily between 1940 and 1970. The decade of the 50s saw a 77.9 percent increase in total land area, which was followed by the 94.7 percent increase during the 1960s. By the 1980s, even the major cities in the south had ceased their rapid expansion. The region most unlike the other regions is the west. Cities in that region continued a relatively aggressive expansion program in the 1980s and accounted for approximately 60 percent of the total square miles annexed to all the sample cities during that period.

Several explanations can be offered to explain the ending of the second wave. In an earlier era, when county government as an institution was less sophisticated, the movement of territory from the county as service provider to the city was easier. However, in the last few decades many county governments that serve primarily unincorporated territory have become more like an urban services deliverer, such that the loss of territory creates significant problems for that county government. The loss of territory also means a loss of income to the county in that the assessed value is lost through the annexation. However, reductions in expenditures for not having to provide that service generally are far less than the revenue loss. Hence, the city's gain is the county's loss. As a result, more resistance is mounted to limit the ability of center cities to annex.

Second, vast areas of many of the rapidly expanding cities are currently undeveloped land. As a result, significant residential, commercial, and industrial development can occur within the existing borders of those cities.

Finally, as the imperial cities of the 19th century learned, so learned the imperial cities of the 20th century: expansion—particularly hostile expansion—invariably leads to protective legislation that makes further expansion more difficult.

City-County Consolidation

A city-county consolidation is exactly that—the governments of the city and of the county are combined into a single government. It captures and embodies the reformist's ideal. For all its promise as a solution to metropolitan problems and all the ink it has received as an idea, its impact on the structure and function of metropolitan America is marginal. During the period 1805–1977, there were only 27 such consolidations, no attempts at consolidation between 1907 and 1947, and only 17 approved by voters out of 83 efforts. Most consolidations involved counties with populations below 100,000. Finally, few occurred in the highly politically diffused midwest and northeast that arguably is most in need of such consolidations (ACIR, 1985).

There is an outlier to the above observations. Recently (November, 2000), the City of Louisville and Jefferson County merged through referendum. As noted earlier, this merger followed a long compact between the two governments that had created a common revenue base and a clear delineation of services for each of the governments. Arguably, this merger represented the first significant city-county consolidation since 1969, when Indianapolis was merged.

Perhaps more importantly, few of the city-county consolidations, including Louisville-Jefferson County, were complete. Most were partial consolidations allowing for territorially based special districts that could continue to provide services (Stephens and Wikstrom, 1999; Kincaid, 1997). Indeed, the Louisville merger left 83 suburban governments and the existing network of small police and fire departments totally intact (Peirce, 2000).

Mergers and Consolidations

Mergers and consolidations occur when two or more municipalities combine to become a single municipality. Historically, as a form of structural regionalism, it was much more prevalent in the 19th century as part of the "imperial" expansion of the larger cities in the eastern United States. Annexation by those cities involved both incorporated and unincorporated territory. Of 38 separate instances of annexations or consolidations involving New York City, Chicago, Philadelphia, Boston, Pittsburgh, Detroit, St. Louis, and Baltimore prior to 1927, 24 of the instances were forced upon the suburban communities and 11 of those instances involved incorporated municipalities (National Municipal League, 1974: 74). More so than with the absorption of unincorporated territory, the forced absorption into the larger city by previously independent municipalities triggered protective legislation that makes involuntary mergers and consolidations extremely difficult. For instance, Pennsylvania laws regarding mergers have been revised to mandate that a positive vote in all municipalities involved in a potential merger must approve that consolidation. As a result, no municipality can be forced to merge or consolidate unless a majority of the voters *in that municipality* agree to that merger or consolidation.

By the time of the second wave of center city expansion after World War II, such protective legislation and the abundance of unincorporated territory available for center cities to expand into has minimized the role of merger or consolidation involving the center city. As a form of struc-

tural regionalism, the consolidation or merger of municipalities not necessarily involving the center city does occur, but on an extremely limited
basis. In 1952, there were 16,778 municipalities in United States. By 1997,
that number had grown to 19,372—a growth of 15.5 percent (U.S. Bureau
of Census, Census of Governments, 1997). Contrasting the growth of
municipalities with that of school districts further emphasizes the limited role of municipal mergers and consolidations. In 1952 there were
56,346 school districts in United States. By 1997, this number had been
reduced to 13,726 (U.S. Bureau of Census, Census of Governments, 1997).

Notes

1. Tax increment financing is an economic development tool that pledges new,
primarily property, taxes generated from the economic expansion to pay for the
capital cost of the infrastructure necessary to support the economic development.
As a result, for the first few years after the development, the local government
taxing body does not see additional tax revenues. However, when those capital
costs have been paid, the additional tax revenues flow to the local government.

2. A correlation statistic [r] is a number that ranges from –1 to +1 and represents
the correlation or association of any two variables. A score of –1 indicates that the
two variables are perfectly correlated in the opposite direction—as one goes up
the other goes down. A score of +1 indicates that the two variables are perfectly
correlated in that they both go up or down in the exact same relationship to each
other. A score of 0 means that there is no relationship between the two variables.

8

Metropolitan Issues

Throughout this book I have attempted to present a balanced and descriptive overview of the governance structure of metropolitan regions in the United States. I think I am able to accomplish that task because, to coin a phase used by the late Billy Martin, controversial and highly opinionated manager of the New York Yankees baseball team, when he was asked whether he liked a sponsor's beverage product because it was "less-filling" or "tastes better," "I feel strongly both ways." There are times when the system appears disjointed, fractionalized, and in need of serious overhaul; yet there are also times when the system works surprisingly well and reflects the norms and values of the citizens it is purported to serve. There are times when my frustrations with managing the City of Pittsburgh have made me long for a unified system of governance; yet there are times when I long to return to my first positive experiences with an engaged civil community as a town manager in a town meeting system.

Consequently, I do not have a closing chapter that synthesizes where the future development of America's metropolitan regions will go. My sense is it will continue to become more diffuse while simultaneously developing more locally defined cooperative strategies. Perhaps "linked or complex networks," as suggested by Savitch and Vogel (2000), is a good descriptor.

Part of the problem of prognostication rests in the absence of good quantitative research methods about metropolitan regions. Syed (1966, 158) lamented that the reason that a theory of local government had not emerged was that theorists relied too heavily on history and "History is the repository of all kinds of lessons. It is a mistress from whose door no suitor returns unrewarded." Unfortunately, the same rules apply to the study of metropolitan regions. One's search will always find the evidence needed to support whatever it was one originally thought to be the case.

Therefore, rather than a synthesis, I want to conclude by suggesting that rigorous research employing new and creative methodologies is necessary to break out of the inconclusiveness that has dominated metropolitan research. Let me offer some methodologies that represent what I mean.

The Role of Metropolitan Structure—Race and Economics

Sorting by Race

In addition to information about regional variations in the diffusion of power and changes in that relationship over time, the MDPI can be used to explain variations in other characteristics of metropolitan regions. For instance, it has been speculated that jurisdictional boundaries are used to sort individuals, by race (Weiher, 1991; Stein 1987).

For this discussion, I will use a feature of the MPDI that isolates the contribution the three major types of local government institutions make to the overall diffusion score. The three institutions are county government, municipal governments, and special districts. Because the MDPI represents the sum of each participating government's contribution to that score, it is easy to identify the contribution by major type of institution. For instance, the Pittsburgh metropolitan region had a 1992 MPDI score of 11.566. County governments within the region contributed .993 to that score; municipalities contributed 7.139 and special districts contributed 3.434.

Harrison and Weinberg (1992) assessed residential segregation in the United States based on nineteen statistical measures. Using measures of evenness, exposure, concentration, centralization and clustering for Blacks, Hispanics, Asians, and Native Americans, they measured 320 metropolitan regions and developed a "dissimilarity index" for those metropolitan areas where the Black, Hispanic, or Asian population exceeded two percent of the total metropolitan population. The "dissimilarity index" focuses on the evenness dimension. It represents a number between 0 and 1 and reflects the percentage of the minority population that would have to move in order to produce a proportional distribution of that minority population across the metropolitan area. A score of "1" would mean that the entire minority population would have to move—a condition of total segregation—while a score of 0 would represent total integration.

We can use this Black dissimilarity index in conjunction with the MPDI to identify the correlation between them. The results are interesting. The 1992 MPDI is significantly correlated with the 1990 Black dissimilarity index with an *r* equal to .493.[1] The Black dissimilarity index is significantly correlated with county government with an *r* equal to .232 and special districts with an *r* equal to .201. Those correlations are not as strong as the one with municipal governments with an *r* equal to .511. That it is strongest with municipal governments makes sense. As general-purpose governments, they are the governments with the zoning and land use controls that can effectively decide who or which groups of individuals can locate within their borders.

As has been suggested by our earlier analysis of the MPDI, it is sensitive to both region-of-states and overall metropolitan population. The above association between the MPDI and Black dissimilarity index needs to be tested against those variables. To accomplish that end, a more rigorous statistical analysis of variance was done with the MPDI, region-of-states, and population as explanatory variables. When that test is performed, each of those variables makes a significant individual contribution to explaining about 33 percent of the variance in Black segregation. Of the three, the MPDI had the highest associational relationship. This means that, even when accounting for population and region, jurisdictional diffusion is significantly and unquestionably linked to Black segregation in metropolitan America. Although there has long been speculation that such a link existed, the validation through the index makes it statistically clear.

As a final test, the Black dissimilarity index was again tested against region-of-states and metropolitan population, but this time only the municipal portion of the MPDI was used. It is this group of local government institutions that have the land use and zoning powers which are the tools that can be used to implement segregationist practices. The results of that test validate the statistical relationship between jurisdictional diffusion and Black segregation.

Knowing that this linkage exists empirically helps to weed through the competing claims for what should be the appropriate design of a metropolitan region. It also suggests that, of a wide number of social ends to be served by diffused, linked governance systems in metropolitan areas, those systems will be weakest in addressing issues of social equity and racial equality. Rather than argue over whether such inequity exits, we should turn our attention to solving the social problem created. It is clear that such addressing will have to be mandated by federal, state, or judicial actions on metropolitan regions. However, precedent now exists. Such requirements to deal with social equity issues are hardly different than those federal, state, and judicial actions that have created metropolitan problem-solving capacity in the areas of environmental and transportation policy. Knowing that local governments having learned or are at least learning how to address metropolitan region issues, the federal, state, and judicial institutions should push those governments into addressing such issues as racial segregation.

Economic Development

Another use of the MPDI has been undertaken by Paytas (2001). Starting with a desire to assess whether the structure of governance in a metropolitan region has any impact on the economic competitiveness of a metropolitan region, Paytas developed a measure of how much of a metropolitan region's economic growth over time was a function of policies controllable by that region. Clearly, large, regional shifts in the United States economy from the rust belt to the sun belt constitute forces that are beyond the control of metropolitan regions in either the northeast or the midwest. However, within those broad regional trends, why do some metropolitan regions experience more economic growth than others? Of particular concern to Paytas was the question of whether the structure of regional governance made a difference.

Currently, work in this area has been anecdotal. Lewis (1996) asserts that suburban development patterns in regions where power is highly concentrated are more apt to have new developments located at highly accessible locations and to be proximate to, or combined with, housing and services. Conversely, new developments in regions where power is highly diffuse will appear at a variety of locations, some with poor accessibility. In addition, there is a likelihood of leapfrog development and a mismatch between jobs and housing.

Although suggestive of a role that structure plays in economic development, Lewis' work does not assess whether one metropolitan governance structure leads to better outcomes as measured by overall economic performance than another. To get at that more important issue, Paytas utilized a technique known as shift-share analysis. Shift-share analysis assumes that changes in employment in a region are a function of national trends, the particular mix of industries in a region and a residual that represents the competitive strength of the local economy. The assumption is that regions that perform better on this overall indicator

Table 8.1 Regional Economic Competitive Scores

| | | State-Local Relations are: | | |
		Centralized	Decentralized	Total
Metropolitan Region is:	Diffused	-0.73	1.64	0.47
	Unified	1.97	5.12	3.67
	Total	0.57	3.44	

SOURCE: *Adapted from Paytas (2001)*

have a healthier, more robust economy and regions that have a high residual represent those that have managed to make their economy more competitive and robust than it would otherwise have been.

In addition to using the MPDI as a measure of the governance structure of the metropolitan region, Paytas also assessed two other features of the metropolitan landscape. The first was whether the metropolitan region also housed the state capital. His assumption was that economies in metropolitan areas where the state capital was located would perform better than others. His analysis suggested that this was not the case. The second feature dealt with the relationship between the state government and the local governments within a particular metropolitan region. As we have discussed, local governments are creatures of their respective state legislatures. The MPDI focuses on the relationships between local governments within a particular metropolitan area. It does not, however, address the issue of the role that the state government plays in defining the scope and responsibilities of local governments within that arena. Based on the work of Stephens (1974), Paytas measured the relative centralization of state-local relations in each of the metropolitan regions.

The results of Paytas' analysis present an interesting picture (see Table 8.1) about how the structure of governance in metropolitan areas affects the economic performance of those areas. In reading Table 8.1, the higher the economic competitive score, the more effective the regions have been in economic development. Initially, the MPDI shows a strong and powerful negative relationship with the portion of economic expansion that can be attributed to local policies. The more diffused (high scores on the MPDI) power is in a metropolitan region, the less likely economic expansion in that region will be a function of local policies. Clearly, highly diffuse metropolitan regions could still see considerable economic expansion. However, that expansion is not as great as it would have been had power been less diffuse. This finding is one of the first efforts to create a quantifiable, statistically significant link between regional structure and economic performance.

Secondly, the analysis demonstrates that, indeed, state-local relations exert a powerful influence on economic competitiveness. Whereas diffusion of metropolitan power is negatively related to economic performance, decentralized state-local relations exerts a positive relationship. The result is that economic performance is best in unified metropolitan regions in decentralized states. Highly diffuse metropolitan regions that operate within a centralized state show the worst ability to affect their local economies. Conversely, less diffuse metropolitan regions will perform better in centralized states. Upon reflection, this observation also makes intuitive sense. Decentralized states, either because the decentralization is designed to place responsibility at the local level or because that decentralization adversely affects economic performance, are not in a position to assist local regional economies. However, more unified metropolitan regions are better able to organize to support economic competitiveness.

Overall, the effect of state centralization is negative. At least historically, power devolved to the local governments within the state creates the necessary condition for greater economic performance. However, when local governments fail to unify that devolved authority at the metropolitan level, the opportunity is lost. This observation may well serve as an important empirical support for the notion that the metropolitan region is, indeed, the right size for the globalization of the economy. Centralized state systems and decentralized metropolitan region systems underperform, in economic development, empowered but more centralized metropolitan regions.

The MPDI is a measure of the political structure of a metropolitan region. We have used it as a tool to explore how government structure affects characteristics of those metropolitan regions. At least in these two analyses, it has suggested that too much diffusion of power in metropolitan areas serves to increase the probability of racial segregation and to deter the ability of the metropolitan region to take advantage of economic expansion occurring within the region.

The Role of Structure—
Maintaining Fiscal Equity between Jurisdictions

I have developed a methodology that allows a government to benchmark itself against other governments to determine its relative standing in the metropolitan region in which it cooperates and competes. I developed this scale for use whether one's personal views are with the "organic whole" or the "polycentric" perspective. Although I will use the scale to demonstrate concerns I have about the implications of the polycentric model, its utility as an assessment tool for local governments is obvious. Hence, it can be used from an academic perspective as it relates to the ongoing debate over the appropriate structure of governance in a metropolitan region or in an applied context laying out a methodology that allows a government to assess itself against its competition.

As I present the model, I will be using Allegheny County in Pennsylvania as the test site. The Pittsburgh region has the distinction of having one of the most diffused systems of local government in the United States. On the MPDI, the region scored a 10.7 in 1972 and an 11.6 in 1992.

Let us first explore the region in more detail. In six counties covering 4,489 square miles and 2,322,938 inhabitants, there are 412 municipalities, 105 school districts, and 332 special districts. Perhaps more important than the number of governments is their small size. Only a few governments represent more than 15,000 people. Overall, 84 percent of all local governments have less than 5,000 inhabitants. Allegheny County, the most populated county in the metropolitan region, covers 727 square miles, has a population of 1.3 million and is served by 296 separate governments and special districts, 128 of which are municipalities.

As the diffused local government system has become more diffuse, its economic structure has changed even more dramatically over the past fifty years. A major element of that change has been the diffusion of the economic base away from the City of Pittsburgh into the former outlying areas of the region. In 1950, 45 percent of the people in Allegheny County lived in the city. In 1990, that percentage was 28 percent. Presently, less than 16 percent of the people in the region live in Pittsburgh.

These population shifts do not fully capture the extent of the economic relocation that has occurred in the region. In 1949, 61 percent of all retail sales and 92 percent of all wholesale trade in Allegheny County took place within the borders of the city. By the mid-80s, those numbers had shrunk to 30 percent and 46 percent, respectively. In the service sector, Pittsburgh's share of economic activity dropped from 75 percent to 51 percent. Including all economic sectors, business volume conducted in Pittsburgh dropped from 73 percent of all 1949 Allegheny County activity to 38 percent of all 1985 business conducted in the county.

The economic transformation of the region is not confined to the center city. To the east and southeast of Pittsburgh, along the banks of the Monongahela River, are 39 municipalities that make up, for lack of a better word, "Mon City." This "city" with a 1990 population of 268,884 has witnessed economic disruption perhaps reminiscent of the 1930's—at least as systematic a disruption in the economy as exists anywhere in urban America. Between 1980 and 1990, 38 of the 39 municipalities experienced population loss; 25 of them by more than 10 percent. Overall, the total population loss was 11.4 percent—comparable to the 12.8 percent loss for the City of Pittsburgh during the same period. "Mon City" is an urban area—percent of families below poverty is almost as high as the City of Pittsburgh, per capita income is actually lower than the city. This economic disruption was not isolated to any one of the 39 municipalities. But the organizational structure that had to deal with the economic disruption included 34 mayors, 272 council members, 12 municipal managers, 38 police departments, 12 school districts, 18 sewage systems, and 36 zoning ordinances.

Given the large number of governments and major changes in the economy, the Allegheny County portion of the region provides an ideal location to test the methodology and assumptions about the effectiveness of competition in a metropolitan region. At least two testable assumptions can be made about the role that competition should be playing. First, although gaps will exist between rich and poor communities, those gaps should be diminishing over time. Even though economic theory might be silent on the issue, citizens of metropolitan areas hold dual citizenship with the state in which the metropolitan regions are located. As such, citizens in all parts of the metropolitan region have some expectation that all will benefit. Second, if competition is working, non-competitive governments should be changing their pricing and product mix to become more competitive. As such, we should be able to see significant changes in the positioning of governments relative to each other as they modify their service bundles.

Following the logic of competition, local elected officials should be and are aware of the competitive marketplace that constitutes the metropolitan landscape of which they are an integral part. This knowledge includes information about costs and services of their government in relation to their neighbors. This is not meant to imply that such information is either accurate or precise. However, it is a form of benchmarking and represents the principle of living in a competitive world.

Elected officials optimize their community's standing and their own personal standing within the community by maximally meeting their constituent demands while minimally taxing their voter-consumers. The

Figure 8.1   Two Dimensional Scale for Identifying Competitive Position of Municipalities in a Metropolitan Region

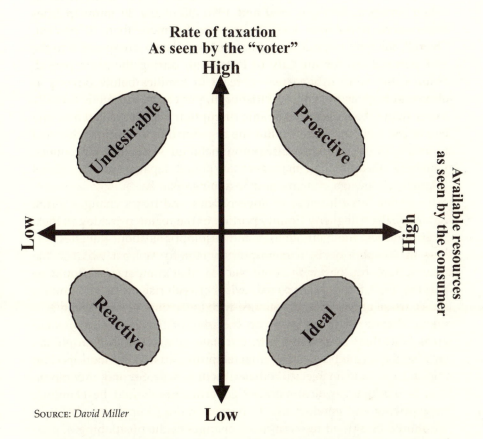

SOURCE: *David Miller*

sought-after result is a bundle of services desired by the consumer and willingly financed by the voter. Indeed, one could envision an ideal state in which the local government taxed the least of any government unit but its citizens received the most.

Conceptualizing the world of local government in this manner suggests a two-dimensional scale (see Figure 8.1). One dimension represents the relative rates of taxation. In the American political culture, the principle of limited government places an important premium on lower rates of taxation. Higher rates of taxation are difficult to defend to the public in their role as "voter." The second dimension represents the resources that are generated from the rates of taxation utilized by a government and adopted by its elected officials. On this dimension, a premium is placed on greater resources as those resources enable the government to address demands for services requested by the public in their role as "consumer."

As is suggested by Figure 8.1, there are four general categories of governments that represent the distribution of governments along this dimensional scale. The first represents those local governments with lower rates of taxation that yield greater resources. These governments would be the envy (or "ideal" as I have categorized them in Figure 8.1) of all the other governments by virtue of having a minimal tax rate for which voters would give credit to their elected officials for "doing their job." These governments would also be envied as the yield from that minimal tax rate would generate substantial dollars for which consumers would give credit to their elected officials for "doing their job."

A second category represents governments that have higher rates of taxation that yield the least resources. Such jurisdictions would be ones that are minimally meeting demands but maximally taxing voter-consumers. These governments and their elected officials would suffer the worst of both worlds. They would be unable to justify the higher rates of taxation to the voter with the delivery of adequate services to the consumer. The "voter" would be upset with the high rates of taxation while the "consumer" would be dissatisfied with the quality of service. Indeed, one could argue that such a jurisdiction is not competitive and, in market terms, constitutes a business failure. I have categorized this group as "undesirable" to represent the difficult position faced by local elected officials. Further, no elected official would seek out this condition. Indeed, identifying communities in this category is the act of identifying fiscally stressed communities.

A third category represents those governments that have higher rates of taxation and those rates of taxation generate relatively higher amounts of resources. I have labeled this category as "proactive." Generally, communities in this category could lower rates of taxation, but service levels appear to be acceptable to voter-consumers. Older, more affluent suburbs may be representative of this category.

The final category represents those governments that have lower rates of taxation and those rates generate relatively lower amounts of resources. Communities in this category could raise their rates of taxation and generate greater resources, but have elected not to do so. Their relatively limited bundle of services appears to be accepted by the voter-consumers. I have labeled this group as "reactive" in that they could, from a resource perspective, address demands, if requested, without creating a non-competitive tax rate. Newer towns on the fringes of an urban area may be representative of this category.

It is possible to operationalize the relative standing of a community in a metropolitan system based on the above analysis. The first dimension can be measured by simply calculating the rate of property taxation of each municipality. Even though similar rates of taxation may generate differing amounts of resources, from a competitive perspective it is assumed that elected officials do compare rates with their neighbors. The second dimension can be measured by estimating the per capita yield generated by those rates of taxation.

An original applied use of this scale was to identify municipalities suffering from fiscal stress. The assumption was that municipalities with the highest rates of taxation and lowest yield from those rates would be the most fiscally stressed in a metropolitan region. These municipalities would be in a condition that would not be one logically chosen by the elected officials. Lacking resources, they would have no reason to design such a package and would be forced into an unacceptable tax package and a resulting inadequate bundle of services. Furthermore, few, if any, voter-consumers would seek out such a community. In the absence of legal authority to go out of business, such communities would nonetheless be non-competitive. Scale economies aside, individuals deciding to locate in these communities would have to contribute more in taxes than they would get back in services in order for the community to improve its fiscal position. As a result, the scale has come to be known as a scale of relative metropolitan fiscal stress.

The methodology for developing the scale is presented below. The first dimension, tax effort, is based on the combined standardized property tax mill rates for each of the county's 128 municipalities. In Pennsylvania, the municipality, the school district in which the municipality is a part, and the county, collect property taxes. Based on the formulas cited above, the 128 municipalities were rank-ordered with the value 1 assigned to the municipality with the highest standardized tax rate. Conversely, the municipality with the lowest standardized tax rate was assigned the value 128.

Resources are measured as the amount of property tax revenue generated per person in the municipality. For each of the 128 municipalities, tax mill rates for municipal, school, and county taxing jurisdictions were multiplied by the assessed value of the community. The resulting number represents the total property tax dollars generated. This number is divided by the community's population to arrive at the total property tax dollars generated per person. Based on the formulas cited above, the 128 municipalities were rank ordered with the value 1 assigned to the municipality with the lowest per capita yield. Conversely, the municipality with the highest per capita yield was assigned the value 128.

A final ranking is calculated by adding together the ranks on the two dimensions. The municipality with the lowest combined score received the rank of 1. The second lowest combined score was assigned the value of 2, and so on until all 128 municipalities received a score.

Low scores indicate a high degree of fiscal stress relative to all the other taxing jurisdictions while higher scores indicate lower degrees of fiscal stress. For instance, the community with the highest overall fiscal stress rating in 1991 was the small borough of Braddock (pop. 4,682). This community had the sixth highest tax effort and third lowest yield of all the municipalities in the county.

For purposes of assessment, the municipalities were divided into quartiles with 32 communities in each group. The 32 communities with the lowest scores were compiled into a group and labeled "stressed." The next 32 communities were compiled into a group labeled "strapped." The City of Pittsburgh fell into this category and was eliminated from subsequent analysis so that the groups would be relatively equal in population size. Hence, only 31 cases are included in this group. Scores on the scale from 65 to 96 were compiled into a group labeled "stable." The municipalities with the highest scores (and therefore lowest fiscal stress) were compiled into a group labeled "stately."

Although attaching labels to the four classes of communities carries subjective connotations, those labels have heuristic value in presenting the subsequent analysis. Indeed, validating both the scale and the subjective labels assigned is important and necessary. With 20 percent of the non-Pittsburgh population in Allegheny County, communities in the "stressed" category have 52 percent of all families in poverty; 53 percent of all violent crimes; and 43 percent of all vacant housing units. The median family income in stressed communities is 50 percent of the median family income in the stately communities. Communities in the "stressed" category have 15 percent of the workforce but 24 percent of the unemployed.

Further, in 1987, Pennsylvania adopted the Municipal Fiscal Disparities Act that serves as a Chapter 11 reorganization process for "bankrupt" municipalities. To date, eight communities have been declared a "distressed municipality" as defined in the act. On the scale,

Table 8.2   Fiscal Stress Rankings of Municipalities in 1981 and 1998

Ranking in 1981	Ranking in 1998				
	Stately	Stable	Strapped	Stressed	Total
Stately	23	7	2		32
Stable	9	13	9	1	32
Strapped		10	13	8	31
Stressed		2	7	23	32
Total	32	32	31	32	127

SOURCE: *Extracted from data from the Commonwealth of Pennsylvania. Department of Community and Economic Development. Local Government Financial Statistics. 1981, 1998*

those municipalities all fall in the "stressed" category. Indeed, they rank first, second, third, fourth, fifth, sixth, eleventh, and twelfth.

One use of the scale is to assess changes in the relative standing of a community over time. Ideally, communities should be moving up the scale. Stressed communities are desirous of becoming unstressed. Conversely, stately communities would certainly want to preserve that standing. Table 8.2 demonstrates just how difficult a task upward movement is. Of the 32 communities categorized as stately in 1981, 23 were still stately in 1998. Conversely, of the 32 stressed communities in 1981, 23 were still stressed 17 years later in 1998.

That there has been so little relative movement of municipalities is disappointing if one assumes the competitive marketplace is working. This finding challenges the assumption that competition serves to motivate the non-competitive to become competitive. That observation notwithstanding, I would like to do a more detailed analysis of the resource side of the scale. This assessment is facilitated by virtue of the relatively equal population distribution in the four categories. Table 8.3 shows population by category for 1981 and 1994. 1994 population ranged from 196,211 in the stressed communities to 263,944 in the stable communities. Overall, the communities in Allegheny County, outside of the City of Pittsburgh, lost 5.8 percent of their population during the decade of the 1980s. Only communities in the stately category showed a modest 2.3 percent population increase. Demographic changes fail to

Table 8.3   Population Change

| | 1981 | 1994 | Change | |
			Number	Percent
Stately	249,211	254,908	5,697	2.3%
Stable	278,589	263,944	(14,645)	(5.3%)
Strapped	272,799	250,794	(22,005)	(8.1%)
Stressed	224,987	196,211	(28,776)	(12.8%)
Total	1,027,566	967,847	(59,719)	(5.8%)

SOURCE: *Extracted from data from the Commonwealth of Pennsylvania. Department of Community and Economic Development. Local Government Financial Statistics. 1981, 1994*

confirm the notion that stressed and strapped communities can become competitive through adjustments to their services. During the study period, they continued on a downward spiral of population loss.

To measure change over time, a measure called a "disparity index" will be utilized. This index is designed to measure the difference between those communities in the stressed category against those communities in the stately category. Ideally, the economic health of communities should be both improving and relatively consistent. Gaps between rich and poor communities will always be part of the metropolitan environment. The very nature of competition among municipalities suggests that differences are normal and healthy. However, the distance between rich and poor should also be minimized or, at least, kept from widening.

Changes in the disparity index demonstrate that, in the Allegheny County case, the gap between the richer and poorer communities is growing—and at an alarming rate. Table 8.4 compares the change in the value of real estate from 1981 to 1997. For purposes of this analysis, the figures have been standardized to 1991 dollars. In 1981, in the stressed communities, there was $2,759 per person of taxable value. By 1991, per capita value had grown by only 9.9 percent to $3,033. For the stately communities, taxable value grew by an inflation-adjusted 69.9 percent from $5,658 to $9,613. The disparity index, as a result, grew from 2.05 to 3.17— a 54.6 percent increase.

The 1991 to 1997 period shows a pattern of similar results such that, over the span of 16 years, stately communities were growing in value at a rate five times faster than the stressed communities. Such a differential

Table 8.4 Comparison of Changes in Per Capita Property Tax Assessments

	Year			Change	
	1981	1991	1997	91-81	97-81
Stately	5,658	9,613	12,312	69.9%	117.6%
Stable	4,496	6,348	7,585	41.2%	68.7%
Strapped	3,317	4,258	4,603	28.4%	38.8%
Stressed	2,759	3,033	3,393	9.9%	23.0%
Disparity Index	2.05	3.17	3.63	54.6%	76.9%

SOURCE: *Extracted from data from the Commonwealth of Pennsylvania. Department of Community and Economic Development. Local Government Financial Statistics. 1981, 1991, 1997.*

growth pattern, absent a corresponding increase in population, reveals a significant redistribution of wealth within the metropolitan area that was exaggerated by the very nature of diffusion itself. The logical conclusion derived from the Allegheny experience is that regional growth will be more disparate if the region itself is fragmented. Because there were so many choices where wealth could go, it selected a few areas at the expense of many areas.

As could be anticipated from the high difference in underlying value between the categories, the rates of taxation are highly differentiated. Lacking value, stressed municipalities are forced to utilize higher rates of taxation to compensate. Table 8.5 compares real estate tax rates for 1981, 1991 and 1997. The formula that was used earlier to categorize municipalities included property tax mill rates from the municipality, school district and county. The mill rates in this section include only those assessed by the municipality. In 1981, the average tax rate for stressed communities was 31.70 mills. The average rate for stately communities was 11.80 mills. The disparity between those two categories was 2.69. That difference held steady and even grew slightly between 1981 and 1991. Stressed communities' average tax rate grew to 37.00 mills while stately communities' average increased to 13.40 mills. Of more interest is the growth of tax rates in the stable and strapped categories—growing 26.3 percent and 22.3 percent respectively. It is likely that these communities were facing greater difficulties in addressing consumer demands than the other categories. Stately communities already had sufficient growth in resources,

Table 8.5   Comparison of Changes in Rates of Real Estate Taxation (in mills)

	Year			Change (Percent)	
	1981	1991	1997	91-81	97-81
Stately	11.80	13.40	12.92	13.6	9.5
Stable	15.60	19.70	18.53	26.3	18.8
Strapped	17.90	21.90	21.07	22.3	17.7
Stressed	31.70	37.00	37.71	16.7	19.0
Disparity Index	2.69	2.76	2.92	2.8	8.6

SOURCE: *Extracted from data from the Commonwealth of Pennsylvania. Department of Community and Economic Development. Local Government Financial Statistics. 1981, 1991, 1997.*

while stressed communities were at the upper limits of what they could legally tax under Pennsylvania law.

The application of the rates of property taxation as reported in Table 8.5 to the valuation of property reported in Table 8.4 provides an estimate of the resources available to municipalities. Those estimates have been divided by the population to generate the per capita yield presented in Table 8.6. In 1981, the high rates of taxation in stressed communities were used to generate more in available resources than in any of the other categories. At $82.40 per person, stressed communities' resources exceeded stately communities' by $17.67. Indeed, the disparity index was actually significantly under 1. The table also shows the significant changes over time in the gap between rich and poor. As previously indicated, tax rate increases in stately communities was half the increase of stressed communities. However, that modest increase in rates, coupled with significant increase in valuations, increased the available resources in stately communities by 140.5 percent. Conversely, stressed communities' resources, with twice the rate of increase, grew by only 36.8 percent during the same period. Overall, the disparity between classes of communities grew 75.7 percent. By 1994, the stressed communities had the highest rates of taxation coupled with the slowest growth in resource yield. The competitive position of stressed communities worsened between 1981 and 1994, explaining why those at the bottom were unable to leave that status.

Let me switch to assessing how those resources are utilized. To assist in that analysis, I have developed a set of expenditures referred to as "core services." Particularly as they relate to Pennsylvania, these represent services that all local governments provide or are expected to provide. This

Table 8.6   Comparison of Changes in Per Capita Municiple Property Taxes

	Year				
	1981	1984	1991	1994	Change (Percent)
Stately	$64.73	$80.73	$127.24	$155.65	140.5
Stable	$67.66	$78.26	$123.03	$149.02	120.3
Strapped	$56.63	$63.42	$92.69	$103.92	83.5
Stressed	$82.40	$88.21	$107.12	$112.77	36.8
Disparity Index	0.79	0.92	1.19	1.38	75.7

SOURCE: *Extracted from data from the Commonwealth of Pennsylvania. Department of Community and Economic Development. Local Government Financial Statistics. 1981, 1991, 1997.*

set includes expenditures for general government, public works, and public safety. As was done earlier, these figures have been converted to per capita estimates.

Total spending for core services is presented in Table 8.7. In 1981, the relative spending between stately and stressed categories was approximately equal. Stately communities were spending $112.62 per capita and stressed communities were spending $115.23 per capita. By 1994, that gap had increased by 34.8 percent. Even though rates of taxation increased 9.5 percent in stately communities and 19.0 percent in stressed communities, stately communities had a 120.8 percent increase in resources compared to a 63.9 percent increase for stressed communities. In other words, stately communities have significantly more resources to address consumer demands while increasing rates of taxation less than any other group. Conversely, stressed communities had to increase rates more than stately communities, yet those rate increases generated little in additional resources to generate services desired by the voter-consumers.

The difference between expenditures on core services and the total of taxes generated represents an approximation of discretionary resources available to local elected officials to address non-core services. I have labeled those resources as "quality of life" expenditures. Local governments and its officials want to address local preferences about the social world articulated by its citizens. Those preferences go beyond administrative overhead, public works and public safety. Whether it is for recreational space, libraries, social service programming, senior citizen services, or any of a wide variety of other activities, having discretionary resources is fundamental to addressing those needs. The purpose of this

Table 8.7 Comparison of Changes in Per Capita Core Services Expenditures

	Year				
	1981	1984	1991	1994	Change (Percent)
Stately	$112.62	$127.54	$212.96	$248.69	120.8
Stable	$93.04	$112.90	$165.02	$202.79	118.0
Strapped	$85.03	$104.93	$146.01	$164.92	94.0
Stressed	$115.23	$120.19	$170.06	$188.80	63.9
Disparity Index	0.98	1.06	1.25	1.32	34.8

SOURCE: *Extracted from data from the Commonwealth of Pennsylvania. Department of Community and Economic Development. Local Government Financial Statistics. 1981, 1991, 1997.*

presentation is not to determine what those expenditures are or their appropriateness. Rather, it is the development of an estimation of the potential resources available.

The results of the analysis (presented in Table 8.8) identify the weakness of the competitive model as it relates to the most distressed metropolitan players. The situation in 1981 was already one where stately communities had more resources to address quality of life issues than stressed communities. Where stressed communities had $9.37 per person, stately communities had $22.68. By 1994, stately communities had $85.40 per person. Not only do stately communities have significantly more resources to do a better job with core services, they have vast resources to deal with other issues of concern to voter-consumers.

Stressed communities, conversely, were redirecting resources away from quality of life expenditures back to core services. Even the redirection of those quality of life resources failed to yield the same increase in core services that other groups enjoyed. And, to make matters worse, stressed communities had to tax the "voter" more to give the "consumer" less.

At a procedural level, the scale has proved to be a helpful methodological tool that would allow local governments to assess their tax and service position against the "competition" in the area in which they are competing. It also suggests that competition between "fiscally healthy" governments may be a reasonable way to organize a metropolitan shopping mall of municipal governments. The problem, as it relates to metropolitan regions, is the plight of the worse-off municipalities. The conceptual base for non-competitive governments becoming competitive is more wishful thinking than theoretically grounded. The data, as suggest-

Table 8.8 Comparison of Changes in Resources Available for Quality of Life Expenses

	Year				Change
	1981	1984	1991	1994	
Stately	$22.68	$39.49	$71.41	$85.40	276.6%
Stable	$25.70	$20.52	$44.28	$43.75	70.2%
Strapped	$6.57	$2.86	$19.97	$11.66	94.0%
Stressed	$9.37	$5.96	$1.07	($1.90)	63.9%

SOURCE: *Extracted from data from the Commonwealth of Pennsylvania. Department of Community and Economic Development. Local Government Financial Statistics. 1981, 1991, 1997.*

ed by this analysis, demonstrates that the conceptual base is simply wrong. Indeed, competition feeds upon itself and makes the competitive more competitive, and the non-competitive more non-competitive.

Summary

Local governments are the building blocks of metropolitan regions and metropolitan regions are the emerging institutions through which decisions about the nature and content of public services will be made. But, as building blocks in an age where governance is a shared responsibility of networks of public, private, and non-profit institutions, they are no longer monopolies. In addition, metropolitan regions may never become a government in the sense of a fixed boundary with clearly defined legislators and executives. Rather, these regions will reflect the governance nature of decision making.

As we look at and assess that governing structure of metropolitan regions, we need to identify the broad purposes for which we desire a particular set of outcomes and what those outcomes are. I would offer the following as a preliminary set of standards:

- Ability to address issues of fairness and equity;
- Efficient delivery of a set of public services;
- Ability of citizens to participate in the process of making decisions about the social world in which they live; and
- Ability to create a competitive region that retains and attracts human and economic capital.

Assessed against those four criteria, the current state of metropolitan regions is checkered. But local governance in America, whether in the old form of intergovernmental relations (Figure 1.1), or the new form of metropolitan regions (Figure 1.2), has never been a science. Rather, it is an art or craft, dabbled in by myriads of institutions with diverse interpretations of those standards. Compared to the past, today's management is probably better than it ever has been. Knowing that does not help in estimating how good it can or should be.

Notes

1. A correlation statistic [r] is a number that ranges from –1 to +1 and represents the correlation or association of any two variables. A score of –1 indicates that the two variables are perfectly correlated in the opposite direction—as one goes up the other goes down. A score of +1 indicates that the two variables are perfectly correlated in that they both go up or down in the exact same relationship to each other. A score of 0 means that there is no relationship between the two variables.

REFERENCES

ACIR (1995). *MPO Capacity: Improving the Capacity of Metropolitan Planning Organizations to Help Implement National Transportation Policies*. Washington D.C.: U.S. Advisory Commission on Intergovernmental Relations.

ACIR (1985). *State and Local Roles in the Federal System*. Washington D.C.: U.S. Advisory Commission on Intergovernmental Relations.

Adams, C. F., H. B. Fleeter, Y. Kim, M. Freeman, and I. Cho (1996). "Flight from Blight and Metropolitan Suburbanization Revisited." *Urban Affairs Review,* 31, pp. 529–543.

Adrian, Charles and M. Fine (1991). *State and Local Politics*. Chicago: Nelson-Hall Publishers.

Arendt, Hannah (1963). *On Revolution*. New York: The Viking Press.

Barber, Benjamin (1995). *Jihad vs. McWorld*. New York: Times Books.

Beach, W. (2000). "Forum: Tax Revenue Sharing Agreements in Michigan." *Government Finance Review,* 16, No. 6, pp. 34–36.

Benjamin (1980). *The Limits of Politics: Collective Goods and Political Change in Post-Industrial Societies*. Chicago: University of Chicago Press.

Berg, B. and P. Kantor (1996). "New York: the Politics of Conflict and Avoidance," in H.V. Savitch and R. K. Vogel, eds, *Regional Politics: America in a Post-City Age,Urban Affairs Annual Review*, 45. Thousand Oaks: Sage Publications.

Berman, D.R. and L.L. Martin (1988). "State-Local Relations: An Examination of Local Discretion." *Public Administration Review,* 48, pp. 637–642.

Blair, G. S. (1986). *Government at the Grassroots*. Pacific Palisades, CA: Palisades Publishers.

Bollens, J. C. (1957). *Special District Government in the United States*. Berkeley: University of California Press.

Bollens, Scott A. (1986). "A Political-Ecological Analysis of Income Inequality in the Metropolitan Area," *Urban Affairs Quarterly,* 22 (Dec. 1986), pp. 221–241.

Bryce, James (1922). *The American Commonwealth*. New York: The MacMillan Company.

Buchanan, James M. (1975). *The Limits of Liberty*. Chicago: University of Chicago Press.

_____. (1987). *Public Finance in Democratic Process: Fiscal Institutions and Individual Choice*. Chapel Hill: University of North Carolina Press.

Burns, N. (1994). *The Formation of Local Governments: Private Values in Public Institutions.* New York: Oxford University Press.

City of Clinton v. The Cedar Rapids and Missouri River Railroad Company. (1868). 24 Iowa 455.

Commonwealth of Pennsylvania. Department of Community and Economic Development. Local Government Financial Statistics. 1981, 1991, 1994, 1997, 1998. Harrisburg.

Dillon, J.F. (1911). *Commentaries on the Law of Municipal Corporations.* Boston: Little-Brown.

Dolan, Drew A. (1990). "Local Government Fragmentation: Does it Drive up the Cost of Government?" *Urban Affairs Quarterly,* 26 (Sept. 1990), pp. 28–45.

Downs, A. (1994). *New Visions for Metropolitan America.* Washington, D.C.: The Brookings Institution.

_____. (1997). "The Devolution Evolution: Congress is Shifting a Lot of Power to the Wrong Levels." *Brookings Policy Brief No. 3.* Washington, D.C.: The Brookings Institution.

Dye, T.R. (1966). *Politics, Economics, and the Public Policy Outcomes in the American States.* Chicago: Rand McNally.

Elazar, D. J. (1975). "Suburbanization: Reviving the Town on the Metropolitan Frontier." *Publius: The Journal Of Federalism,* 5, No. 1, pp. 53–80.

_____. (1966). *American Federalism: A View from the States.* New York: Thomas Crowell.

_____. (1971). "Community Self-Government and the Crisis of American Politics." *Ethics,* pp. 91–106.

Fabricant, S. (1952). *The Trend of Government Activity in the United States Since 1900.* New York: National Bureau of Economic Research, Inc.

Foster, K. A. (1997). "Regional Impulses." *Journal of Urban Affairs,* 19, No. 4, pp. 375–403.

Fredrickson, H.G., C. Wood and B. Logan (2001). "How American Governments Have Changed: The Evolution of the Modern City Charter." *National Civic Review,* 90, No. 1, pp. 3–18.

Frey, Bruno (1978). *Modern Political Economy.* New York: Wiley.

Friedman, J. and J. Miller (1965). "The Urban Field." *Journal of the American Institute of Planner, pp.* 312–320.

Friesma, H. Paul (1971). *Metropolitan Political Structure; Intergovernmental Relations and Political Integration in the Quad-Cities.* Iowa City: University of Iowa Press.

Frug, G. (1980). "The City as a Legal Concept." *Harvard Law Review,* 93, pp. 1059–1154.

_____. (1999). *City Making: Building Communities Without Building Walls.* Princeton, NJ: Princeton University Press.

Garn, Harvey A. and Michael Springer (1975). "Formulating Urban Growth Policies: Dynamic Interactions Among People, Places, and Clubs." *Publius: The Journal of Federalism,* 5, No.4, pp. 25–49.

Garreau, Joel (1992). *Edge City: Life in the New Frontier.* NY: Anchor Books.

Gere, E.A. (1982). "Dillon's Rule and the Cooley Doctrine: Reflections on the Political Culture." *Journal of Urban History,* 8, pp. 271–298.

Gilbertson, H.S. (1917). *The County, the Dark Continent of American Politics.*

American Short Ballot Association.

Goodman, J.S. (1980). *The Dynamics of Urban Growth and Politics.* New York: Macmillan.

Halloway, W. V. (1951). *State and Local Government in the United States.* New York: McGraw-Hill.

Hamilton, D. (1998). "Organizing Government Structure and Governance Functions in Metropolitan Areas in Response to Growth and Change: A Critical Overview." *Journal of Urban Affairs,* 22, No.1, pp. 65 – 84.

Hansberry, J. (2000). "Denver's Scientific and Cultural Facilities District: A Case Study in Regionalism." *Government Finance Review,* 16, No. 6, pp. 13–16.

Hansell, W. (2000). "Evolution and Change Characterize Council-Manager Government." *Public Management,* 82, No. 8, pp. 17–21.

Harrison, Roderick J. and Daniel H. Weinberg (1992). "Racial and Ethnic Segregation in 1990." Washington, D.C.: U.S. Bureau of the Census.

Hawkins, B. W. (1971). *Politics and Urban Policies.* Indianapolis: Bobbs-Merrill Co.

Henton, D., J. Melville and K. Walesh (1997). *Grassroots Leaders for a New Economy: How Civic Entrepreneurs are Building Prosperous Communities.* San Francisco: Jossey-Bass Publishers.

Hill, R.C. (1974). "Separate and Unequal: Governmental Inequality." *The American Political Science Review,* 68, pp.1557–68.

Hitchings, Benjamin G. "A Typology of Regional Growth Management Systems." *The Regionalist,* 3, Nos. 1 and 2. (Fall 1998), pp.1–14.

Hobbes, T. (1964). *Leviathan, Abridged Edition.* New York: Washington Square Press.

Hofstadter, R. (1948). *The American Political Tradition and the Men Who Made It.* New York: Vintage Books.

Hollis, L.E. (1998). "Revenue Sharing and Regional Cooperation: An Urban Land Institute Policy Forum." ULI Public Policy Forum Series, No. 662. Washington: Urban Land Institute.

Hooker, G.E. (1917). "City Planning and Political Areas." *National Municipal Review* (May), pp. 337–345.

Hueglin, Thomas O. (1976). *Early Modern Concepts for a Late Modern World: Althusius on Federalism.* Waterloo, Ont.: Wilfrid Laurier University Press.

ICMA (1996) *The Municipal Yearbook–1996.* Washington: International City and County Management Association.

ICMA. (1984) *The Municipal Yearbook–1984.* Washington: International City Management Association.

Jacobs, Philip E. and James V. Toscano (1964). *The Integration of Political Communities.* Philadelphia: J.B. Lippincott Company.

Jensen, B. And J. Turner (2000). "Act 77: Revenue Sharing in Allegheny County." *Government Finance Review,* 16, No. 6, pp. 17–21.

Jillson, C. C. (1988). "Political Culture and the Patterns of Congressional Politics under the Articles of Confederation." *Publius: The Journal of Federalism,* 18, pp. 1–26.

Keating, Michael (1995). "Size, Efficiency, and Democracy: Consolidation, Fragmentation, and Public Choice," in. David Judge, Gary Stoker, and Harold Wolman, eds., *Theories of Urban Politics, pp.* 117–134.

Kincaid, J. (1980) "Political Culture of the American Compound Republic."

Publius:The Journal of Federalism, 10, pp. 1–16.

_____. (1997). "Regulatory Regionalism in Metropolitan Areas: Voter Resistance and Reform Persistence." http://www.law.pace.edu/landuse/kincaid.html

Langrod, G. (1953). "Local Government and Democracy." *Public Administration,* 31, pp. 83–116.

Ledebur, Larry and W. Barnes (1992). *Metropolitan Disparities and Economic Growth: City Distress and the Need for a Federal Local Growth Package* (research report on America's cities). Washington D.C.: National League of Cities.

_____ (1993). *All In It Together: Cities, Suburbs and Local Economic Regions.* Washington D.C.: National League of Cities.

Lewis, P.G. (1996). *Shaping Suburbia: How Political Institutions Organize Development.* Pittsburgh: University of Pittsburgh Press.

Lineberry, R. L. and E. P. Fowler (1967). "Reformism and Public Policy in American Cities." *American Political Science Review,* 61, pp. 701–716.

Locke, J. (1955). *Of Civil Liberty, Second Treatise.* South Bend, IN: Gateway Edition.

Long, N. (1978). "Regionalism Toward the Year 2000." in Kent Mathewson, ed., *The Regionalist Papers: Toward Metropolitan Unity.* Detroit: The Metropolitan Fund.

Luce, Thomas (1997). "Tax Base Sharing: Simulations of the Twin Cities Model for the Chicago, Philadelphia, Portland, and Seattle Metropolitan Areas." *National Tax Association 1997 Annual Conference Proceedings.*

_____ (1998). "Regional Tax Base Sharing: the Twin Cities Experience." in H.F. Ladd, ed., *Local Government Tax and Land Use Policy.* Washington: Edward Elgar Publishing.

Luria, D. D. and J. Rogers (1999). *Metro Futures: Economic Solutions for Cities and their Suburbs.* Boston: Beacon Press.

Lyons, W. (1978). "Reform and Response in American Cities: Structure and Policy Reconsidered." *Social Science Quarterly,* 59 pp. 118–132.

Maas, A. (1959). *Area and Power: A Theory of Local Government.* New York: The Free Press.

MacKenzie, W. J. (1961). *Theories of Local Government.* London: London School of Economics and Political Science.

Mansbridge, J. J. (1980). *Beyond Adversarial Democracy.* New York: Basic Books.

Marando, V. and R. Thomas (1977). *The Forgotten Governments.* Gainesville: The University Press of Florida.

McGinnis, M. D. ed. (1999). *Polycentricity and Local Political Economies: Readings from the Workshop in Political Theory and Policy Analysis.* Ann Arbor: University of Michigan Press.

McKenzie, E. (1994). *Privatopia: Homeowner Associations and the Rise of Residential Private Governments.* New Haven: Yale University Press.

McQuaid, K., M. Bok, D. Y. Miller and J. James (1992). *Tax Base Sharing as an Alternative Fiscal Policy in Pennsylvania.* Harrisburg: Center for Rural Pennsylvania.

Mill, John Stuart (1873). *Considerations on Representative Government.* New York: Henry Holt and Company.

Miller, D. Y. and C. M. DeLoughry (1996). *1995 Organizational Assessment: A*

Report to the Southwestern Pennsylvania Regional Planning Commission. Pittsburgh: The Pennsylvania Economy League.

Miller, D. Y., R. Miranda, R. Roque, and C. Wilf (1995). "The Fiscal Organization of Metropolitan Areas: The Allegheny County Case Reconsidered." *Publius: The Journal of Federalism,* 25, No. 4, pp. 19–36.

Miller, D.Y. (1988). *Political Culture and Other Determinants of State and Local Government Expenditures in the United States.* Pittsburgh: University of Pittsburgh.

_____. (1991). "The Impact of Political Culture on Patterns of State and Local Government Expenditures. " *Publius: The Journal of Federalism,* 21, No. 2, pp. 83–100.

_____. (1999). "Transforming the Governance of Western Pennsylvania from Town to Region." in Ralph Bangs, ed., *The State of the Region. Economic, Demographic, and Social Conditions and Trends in Southwestern Pennsylvania. .* Pittsburgh: University Center for Social and Urban Research, University of Pittsburgh.

_____. (2000). "Fiscal Regionalism: Metropolitan Reform without Boundary Changes." *Government Finance Review,*16, No. 6, pp. 7–11.

Minnesota House of Representative's Research Department (1987). *Minnesota's Fiscal Disparities Program: Tax Base Sharing in the Twin Cities Metropolitan Area, A Research Report.*

Mitchell-Weaver, C., D.Y. Miller and R. Deal (2000). "Multilevel Governance and Metropolitan Regionalism in the USA." *Urban Studies,* 37, No. 5–6, pp. 851–876.

Mosher, F. (1982). *Democracy and the Public Sector.* New York: Oxford University Press.

Mueller, Dennis C. (1979). *Public Choice.* Cambridge: Cambridge University Press.

Mumford, Lewis (1961). *The City in History.* New York: The Free Press.

Nalbandian, J. (1991). *Professionalism in Local Government: Transformations in the Roles, Responsibilities, and Values of City Managers.* San Francisco: Jossey-Bass.

National Association of Regional Councils. Website: http://www.narc.org/

National Municipal League, Committee on Metropolitan Government (1974). *The Government of Metropolitan Areas in the United States.* New York: Arno Press.

National Research Council, Committee on Improving the Future of U. S. Cities Through Improved Metropolitan Area Governance (1999). *Governance and Opportunity in Metropolitan America.* Washington DC: National Academy Press.

Office of Management and Budget (1999). *OMB Bulletin No. 99–04.*

Orfield, Myron (1997*). Metro-Politics: A Regional Agenda for Community Stability.* Washington D.C.: Brookings Insitution.

Orum, Anthony M. (1991). "Apprehending the City: the View from Above, Below, and Behind." *Urban Affairs Quarterly* 26, No. 4, pp. 581–609.

Ostrom, E. (1972). "Metropolitan Reform: Propositions Derived from Two Traditions." *Social Science Quarterly,* 53, pp. 474–493.

Ostrom, V., C. M. Tiebout and R. Warren (1961). "The Organization of Government in Metropolitan Areas: A Theoretical Inquiry." *American Political Science Review,* 55, pp. 831–842.

Parks, Roger B. and Ronald J. Oakerson (1992). *Metropolitan Organization: The Allegheny County Case.* Prepared for the Advisory Commission on Intergovernmental Relations. Washington, D.C., Feb. 1992.

Paytas, J. (2001). *Governance and Competitive Regions.* Pittsburgh: Graduate School of Public and International Affairs.

Peirce, N. (1993). *Citi-States: How Urban America Can Prosper in a Competitive World.* Washington: Seven Locks Press.

_____. (2000). "Louisville Votes Merger—First Since Indy in 1969." *County News Online—December 18, 2000.* Washington: National Association of Counties. http://countynews.org

Peterson, Paul E. (1979). "A Unitary Model of Local Taxation and Expenditure Policies in the United States." *British Journal of Political Science,* 9, pp. 281–314.

_____. (1981). *City Limits.* Chicago: University of Chicago Press.

Porter, M.E. (1998). "Clusters and the New Economics of Competition." *Harvard Business Review,* November-December, pp. 77–90.

Rawls, John (1972). *A Theory of Justice.* Oxford: Clarendon Press.

Reed, T.H. (1925). "The Region, a New Governmental Unit: The Problem of Metropolitan Areas." *National Municipal Review,* XIV (July). pp. 417–423.

Riley, P. (1976). "Three 17th Century German Theorists of Federalism: Althusius, Hugo, and Liebnitz." *Publius: The Journal of Federalism,* 6, No.3, pp. 7–42.

Roundtable on Regional Planning (1926). *The American Political Science Review,* XX, pp. 156–163.

Rusk, D. (1993). *Cities without Suburbs.* Baltimore: Johns Hopkins Press.

Rusk, D. (1999). *Inside Game Outside Game: Winning Strategies for Saving Urban America.* Washington DC: The Brookings Institution.

Savitch, H., D. Collins, D. Sanders, and J. Markham (1993). "Ties that Bind: Central Cities, Suburbs, and the New Metropolitan Region." *Economic Development Quarterly,* 7, No. 4, pp. 341–357.

Savitch, H. V. and R. K. Vogel (1996). "Louisville and Antagonistic Cooperation, in H. V. Savitch and R. K. Vogel, eds., *Regional Politics: America in a Post City Age* (New York: Sage Publications) pp. 130 – 157.

_____. (2000). "Paths to New Regionalism" *State and Local Government Review,* 32, No.3, pp. 159–168.

Schambra, W. A. (1982). "The Roots of the American Public Philosophy." *Public Interest,* 67, pp. 36–48.

Scherer, F.M. and David Ross (1990). *Industrial Market Structure and Economic Performance.* Boston: Houghton Mifflin Co.

Schneider, M. and K.O. Park (1989). "Metropolitan Counties as Service Delivery Agents: The Still Forgotten Governments." *Public Administration Review,* July/August, pp.345–352.

Schneider, M. (1989). *The Competitive City: The Political Economy of Suburbia.* Pittsburgh: University of Pittsburgh Press.

Sharkansky, I. (1969). "The Utility of Elazar's Political Culture: A Research Note." *Polity*,2, pp. 66–83.

Shepherd, William G. (1985). *The Economics of Industrial Organization.* New Jersey: Prentice Hall.

Smith, B.C. (1985). *Decentralization:The Territorial Dimension of the State.* London: George Allen and Unwin.

Sparrow, G. and L. McKenzie (1983). "Metropolitan Organization: A Theory and Agenda for Research." *National Civic Review,* October, pp. 489–496.

Stein, R. (1987). "Tiebout's Sorting Hypothesis." *Urban Affairs Quarterly,* 23, pp. 140–160.

Stephens, G. Ross (1974). "State Centralization and the Erosion of Local Autonomy." *Journal of Politics,* 36, pp. 44–76.

Stephens, G. Ross and N. Wikstrom (1999). *Metropolitan Government and Governments: Theoretical Perspectives, Empirical Analysis, and the Future.* New York: Oxford University Press.

Stillman, R.J. (1974). *The Rise of the City Manager.* Alberquerque: University of New Mexico Press.

Svara, J. (2001). "Do We Still Need Model Charters? The Meaning and Relevance of Reform in the Twenty-First Century." *National Civic Review,* 90, No. 1, pp. 19–34.

Syed, A. (1966). *The Political Theory of the American Local Government.* New York: Random House.

Tableman, B. (1951*). Governmental Organization in Metropolitan Areas.* Ann Arbor: University of Michigan Press.

Teaford, J. (1979). *City and Suburb: the Political Fragmentation of Metropolitan America, 1850–1970.*

Thomas, R.D. and V. L. Marando (1981). "Local Government Reform and Territorial Democracy." *Publius: The Journal of Federalism,* 11, pp. 49–63.

Tiebout, Charles M. (1956). "A Pure Theory of Local Expenditures." *The Journal of Political Economy.* Chicago: University of Chicago Press.

Tocqueville, A. de (1953). *Democracy in America.* New York: Alfred A. Knopf.

Tregoning, H. (1998). *Becoming Regional: A Federal Role.* Smart Growth Network: http://www.smartgrowth.org/library/tregoning_ground.html

U.S. Advisory Commission on Intergovernmental Relations (1992). *State and Local Roles in the Federal System.* Washington: ACIR.

U.S. Department of Commerce, Bureau of Census. (1982). *Census of Governments. Finance Summary Statistics.*

U.S. Department of Commerce, Bureau of Census. (1996). *Census of Governments. Finance Summary Statistics.*

U.S. Department of Commerce, Bureau of Census. (1992). *Census of Governments. Finance Statistics (Preliminary).* CD-ROM. Washington D.C. April 1996

U.S. Department of Commerce, Bureau of Census. (1977). *Census of Governments. Volume 1: Government Organization.*

U.S. Department of Commerce, Bureau of Census. (1997). *Census of Governments. Volume 1: Government Organization.*

U.S. Department of Commerce, Bureau of Census. (1975). *Census of Governments.*

1972: Government Employment and Finance Files (Computer File) ICPSR ed. Ann Arbor, MI: Inter-university Consortium for Political and Social Research (Producer & Distributor).

Walker, D. B. (1986). "Intergovernmental Relations and the Well-Governed City." *National Civic Review,* March/April.

Weiher, Gregory R. (1991). *The Fractured Metropolis: Political Fragmentation and Metropolitan Segregation.* Albany: State University of New York Press.

Wickwar, Hardy W. (1970). *The Political Theory of Local Government.* Columbia: University of South Carolina Press.

Wirt, F. (1985). "The Dependent City? External Influences upon Local Control." *Journal of Politics,* 47, pp. 83–112.

_____. (1991). "Soft Concepts and Hard Data: A Research Review of Elazar's Political Culture." *Publius: The Journal of Federalism,* 21, No. 2, pp. 1–14.

Zeigler, Donald J. and Stanley D. Brunn (1980). "Geopolitical Fragmentation and the Pattern of Growth and Need: Defining the Cleavage Between Sunbelt and Frostbelt Metropolises," in Stanley D. Brunn and James O. Wheeler, eds., *The American Metropolitan System: Present and Future.* London: V.H. Winston and Sons, pp. 77–92.

Zimmerman, J. (1984). "New England Town Meeting: Pure Democracy in Action?" *The Municipal Yearbook 1984.* Washington, D.C.: International City Management Association. pp. 102–106.

_____. (1983). *State-Local Relations: A Partnership Approach.* New York: Praeger Publishers.

Zuckerman, M. (1970). *Peaceable Kingdoms: the New England Towns of the 18th Century.* New York: Norton.

INDEX